INSIDE

★★★★ YOUR MATCH ANNUAL 2018! ★★

★★★★★★★★★★★★★★★★★★★★★★★★★

ALL-TIME PREM DREAM TEAM 40

DELE'S THE MAN!

MATCH is predicting massive things for ENGLAND and TOTTENHAM star Dele Alli in 2018! Here's why we love the world-class wonderkid!

BEST MATES!

TROPHY TIME?

GOAL KING!

BARGAIN OF THE CENTURY!

FACTPACK

DELE ALLI 4

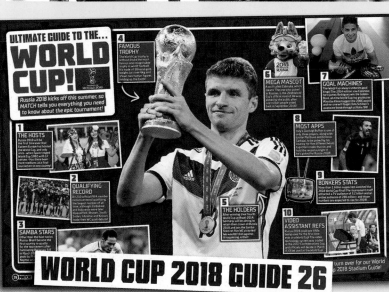

ULTIMATE GUIDE TO THE... WORLD CUP!

Russia 2018 kicks off this summer, so MATCH tells you everything you need to know about the epic tournament!

1. THE HOSTS
2. QUALIFYING RECORD
3. SAMBA STARS
4. FAMOUS TROPHY
5. THE HOLDERS
6. MEGA MASCOT
7. GOAL MACHINES
8. MOST APPS
9. BONKERS STATS
10. VIDEO ASSISTANT REFS

WORLD CUP 2018 GUIDE 26

ULTIMATE TEAM LEGENDS EXPLAINED!

With the release of brand-new FUT Icons on FIFA 18, MATCH takes a closer look at what made some past Legends on FIFA's Ultimate Team so legendary!

SCHOLES
CANNAVARO
CRESPO
FIGO
BEST
NESTA
LINEKER

FUT LEGENDS 78

FOOTY STARS AS KIDS

MATCH blows the dust off some ancient photo albums and raids footy stars' Instagram pages to reveal what they looked like when they were younger!

DANIEL STURRIDGE LIVERPOOL
CHRISTIAN ERIKSEN TOTTENHAM
PAUL POGBA MAN. UNITED
HARRY KANE TOTTENHAM
MARIO GOTZE BORUSSIA DORTMUND
DAVID DE GEA MAN. UNITED
AARON RAMSEY ARSENAL

FOOTY STARS AS KIDS 62

DELE'S THE MAN!

GOAL KING!

Dele's goalscoring ability is out of this world, and he's got Frank Lampard's record tally of Premier League goals for a midfielder in his sights! The ex-Chelsea hero is over 100 ahead, but with Alli's top-class movement and timing, plus his deadly finishing, MATCH reckons he can get close to him!

BARGAIN OF THE CENTURY!

With transfer spending going absolutely crazy in 2017, you'll struggle to find a better bargain than Alli! He cost Tottenham just £5 million when he joined back in 2015, but his value has shot up thanks to his epic performances. If he moved clubs now, it would be for at least £100 million!

BEST MATES!

Off the pitch, the Tottenham CAM's got a proper bromance with team-mate Eric Dier, and as a combination they're hilarious! On the pitch, his partnership with Harry Kane is absolutely lethal too! They're one of the best attacking combos in Europe for both England and Spurs!

TROPHY TIME?

Dele stars for two teams well overdue some silverware. Spurs have bagged just two EFL Cups since he was born, and haven't lifted the title for over 50 years, while England have waited just as long for a trophy! With Alli, we think his club and country's years of hurt will come to an end soon!

FACTPACK

Name: Dele Alli

Club: Tottenham

Country: England **Age:** 21

Position: Att. midfielder

Boots: adidas ACE 17+

RON THE RECORD BREAKER!

CRISTIANO RONALDO shattered loads of records over the past 12 months! MATCH takes a closer look at his mind-blowing year...

THE INVINCIBLES!

Ronaldo was part of the Real Madrid team that went a Spanish record 40 games unbeaten at the start of 2017!

UNSELFISH RON!

CR7's more famous for scoring goals, but he became the Champions League's all-time top creator back in February with his 31st assist!

BONKERS STATUE!

Ron scored his 70th goal for Portugal in March, then got his own statue made at Madeira Airport in his hometown!

GOAL MACHINE!

He beat Jimmy Greaves' 46-year record of 367 league goals to become the all-time leading scorer in Europe's top five divisions!

TON UP!

C-Ron hit a hat-trick in the Champions League semi-finals against Bayern to become the first player to score 100 CL goals!

ANOTHER GOAL, ANOTHER RECORD!

CASH CRAZY!

Cristiano was named the richest athlete on the planet for the second year in a row, pocketing a monster £72m!

HORROR HAIR!

What was Atletico's Antoine Griezmann thinking when he dyed his hair blue last summer?

I'VE GOT CASH TO BURN!

MEGA BUCK$!

Ezequiel Lavezzi earns a mind-blowing £798,000 a week at Hebei China Fortune - the highest salary of any footballer on the planet!

TROPHY HUNTER!

Ex-PSG ace Maxwell won a bonkers 36 club trophies during his epic career - more than any player ever. Mad!

600-MAN!

His double in the Champions League final v Juventus took his career goal tally for club and country to 600. Wow, just wow!

MY TROPHY CABINET IS FULL UP!

SOCIAL MEDIA STAR!

Cristiano's a hero as much off the pitch as he is on it, and he proved it by becoming the first footballer to hit 100 million Instagram followers!

CUP COLLECTOR!

He ended an awesome season by winning the double as Real Madrid bagged the La Liga title and Champions League!

FIFA COVER STAR!

Ronaldo was confirmed as FIFA's cover star for the first time ever when EA revealed their new packshot for FIFA 18!

WORLD CUP STAT ATTACK!

Get a load of the coolest World Cup stats ahead of this summer's big kick-off!

5

Brazil have won the World Cup a record five times, and have also won more games and played in more tournaments than any other country!

16
Germany's Miroslav Klose is the World Cup's all-time top scorer with 16 goals - one ahead of Brazil's legendary net-buster Ronaldo!

2,217

Italy legend Paolo Maldini has played more minutes at the World Cup than any player! He starred in four tournaments between 1990 and 2002!

3
Geoff Hurst is the only player in history to score a hat-trick in a World Cup final! He fired England to glory with a famous treble in 1966!

17

Pele was 17 years old at World Cup 1958 - he became the youngest ever scorer, youngest player to hit a hat-trick and youngest star to net in a final!

DID YOU KNOW?

When Brighton and Huddersfield kicked off their seasons in August, they took the number of clubs to have played in the Prem to 49!

THREE LIONS LEGENDS!

Nine of the ten top Prem scorers ever are English - Shearer, Rooney, Cole, Lampard, Fowler, Defoe, Owen, Ferdinand and Sheringham! Thierry Henry's the only non-Englishman!

YOUNG LIONS ROAR!

ENGLAND's youth teams had an epic summer in 2017, with three of them bagging major trophies! MATCH has picked out a few Young Lions who could be knocking on Gareth Southgate's door very soon!

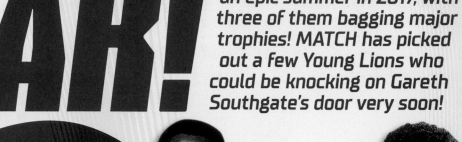

RUSSIA HERE I COME!

STEP ASIDE, KANE!

TAMMY ABRAHAM

Position: Striker Age: 19

Out of all these Young Lions, we reckon U21 hitman Tammy has the best chance of earning a full call-up soon! The goal king ripped it up on loan for Bristol City last season, and will be hoping 2017-18 will be his breakthrough Prem season at Swansea! Parent club Chelsea rate him so highly, they recently gave the lethal finisher a new five-year contract. Hero!

RYAN SESSEGNON

Position: Left-back Age: 17

Fulham wonderkid Sessegnon is not just one of the hottest prospects in England, but on the planet! The speedy dribbler racked up 26 league appearances in 2016-17 for the Championship club, despite only being 16 when the season started! He bombed up and down the Young Lions U19s' left flank as they won the European Championship, too!

DOMINIC SOLANKE

Position: Striker Age: 20

Ice-cool striker Solanke was crucial in England U20s' World Cup victory - he hit four goals and bagged the tournament's Golden Ball! The Liverpool new boy is in good company for that award - previous winners include Lionel Messi, Paul Pogba and Sergio Aguero! Reds fans will be rubbing their hands with glee at the potential of the ex-Chelsea hitman!

STARS' CARS!

Check out these flash wheels and the footy heroes who drive them!

SANCHEZ

Lamborghini Huracan
0-60: 2.5 seconds Price: £155,400

BENZEMA

Ferrari 488 Spider
0-60: 3 seconds Price: £204,400

ADEMOLA LOOKMAN

Position: Forward Age: 19

Just behind Solanke in the goal rankings at the U20 World Cup with three strikes was Everton speed machine Lookman! The highly-rated Toffees teen isn't all about ripping nets, though – his quick bursts of pace and dynamite dribbling skills make him a nightmare to defend against! He's the kind of player who gets supporters off their seats in excitement!

NEXT TROPHY... THE WORLD CUP!

HARVEY BARNES

Position: Att. midfielder Age: 19

You need to keep an eye on this kid! The Toulon Tournament Golden Boot winner can play in midfield or up front thanks to his awesome footy brain! The Leicester hero bagged MK Dons' Young Player Of The Year in 2016-17 - even though he joined the League One club halfway through the season - and now he's on loan in the Championship with Barnsley!

CELEBRITY FANS!

MATCH reveals which clubs these famous celebs support!

CRAIG DAVID
R'n'B hero
Southampton

ADELE
Pop star
Tottenham

ANTHONY JOSHUA
Boxing ledge
Watford

PATRICK STEWART
Ace actor
Huddersfield

LEWIS HAMILTON
F1 speedster
Arsenal

ARCTIC MONKEYS
Top band
Sheff. Wed.

DR. DRE
Rap legend
Liverpool

MICHAEL CAINE
Acting God
Chelsea

HERE COMES 2018!

There's loads of stuff to get excited about in 2018! MATCH looks ahead to another quality year of football...

WORLD CUP CRAZY!

We're buzzing for a huge festival of footy this summer, as Russia hosts the 2018 World Cup! It could be the last time we see legends like Lionel Messi, Cristiano Ronaldo and Andres Iniesta at a WC, while wonderkids like Dele Alli and Kylian Mbappe will make their World Cup bows. Most importantly, it's a whole month of football - GET IN!

MEGA TRANSFERS!

Transfer fees have been getting crazier and crazier, and MATCH reckons more money than ever will get spent this year! Superstars like Harry Kane, Paulo Dybala and Gareth Bale could all come close to Neymar's world-record £200 million fee if they move clubs in 2018!

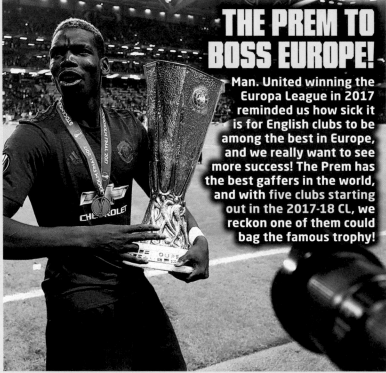

THE PREM TO BOSS EUROPE!

Man. United winning the Europa League in 2017 reminded us how sick it is for English clubs to be among the best in Europe, and we really want to see more success! The Prem has the best gaffers in the world, and with five clubs starting out in the 2017-18 CL, we reckon one of them could bag the famous trophy!

AWESOME TITLE RACE!

MATCH has never found it harder to predict the Premier League title winners than this season! We reckon all top six clubs have the quality to lift the famous trophy, so it could go right down to the wire! Bring on the best title fight ever!

BALLON D'OR BATTLE!

The annual competition between Lionel Messi and Cristiano Ronaldo could be all change next year! With the two top stars both into their 30s now, 2018 could be the year another hero wrestles the Ballon d'Or away from them! Or, it could just end up being another stellar year for the two megastars...

MATCH!
THE BEST FOOTBALL MAGAZINE!

OZIL

FAB FACT
Ozil won Germany's Player Of The Year award five times in six years between 2011 and 2016. Total legend!

BOOTS
adidas ACE 17+

STAT ATTACK
The classy Arsenal midfielder assisted a goal in seven games on the bounce in 2015 - that's a Prem record!

TRANSFER VALUE

£60 MILLION

2018'S A BIG YEAR FOR...
NEYMAR

Can the world's most expensive player prove his worth?

THE STORY SO FAR...

Neymar was well known around the world as a teenager when he burst onto the scene with Santos as a sensational 17-year-old! The youngster turned down offers from Real Madrid and Chelsea to stay with the club, and scored 136 goals in 225 games!

After four years of tearing up Brazilian footy, Barcelona signed Neymar in 2013. A year later, Luis Suarez followed him through the Nou Camp door to form MSN – the deadliest attacking trio ever! Between them, they won two La Ligas and the Champions League!

Last summer was packed with transfer speculation, and after weeks of gossip, NJR stunned the footy world by joining PSG for £200 million! The forward wants to be the main man at a new club to have a chance of winning the Ballon d'Or – can he pull it off?

PRINCE OF PARIS

A big part of Neymar's decision to leave Barcelona was wanting to move out of Lionel Messi's shadow and become the talisman for a new club. PSG were the obvious choice – they're ambitious and will build the team around him! He has to deliver on his price tag, too - his new club will be expecting 20+ league goals, as well as bagging them Ligue 1!

BRAZILIAN HERO

2018 is a massive year for Neymar on the international stage, with the World Cup in Russia to look forward to. As captain of the most successful team in the competition's history, the pressure is seriously on the No.10 to deliver! Brazil is still hurting from humiliation on home soil in 2014, so they'll be looking to their skipper to lead them to glory!

CL CHALLENGE

Neymar was the difference between PSG and Barça when they met in the CL last season, with a stunning double at the Nou Camp to dump his new club out of the tournament! But now he's joined the class of Marco Verratti, Edinson Cavani and Angel Di Maria, the globe's most expensive player will expect to take the French giants to the CL semi-finals at least!

BALLON D'OR BID

In the last 20 years, four Brazilians have been named the world's best player, and Neymar is desperate to follow in the footsteps of Ronaldo, Rivaldo, Ronaldinho and Kaka! If he has a mind-blowing year for club and country, bagging tons of trophies along the way, he'll definitely be one of the hot faves to win the Ballon d'Or!

2018 IN NUMBERS...

10
If he scores six goals at the WC, he'll reach double figures at the tournament!

150
28 Ligue 1 goals this season will take him to 150 league goals in his career!

77
NJR is closing in on Pele's record of 77 goals for Brazil!

11
He'll be the first Brazilian to win the Ballon d'Or in 11 years if he bags the 2018 award!

KYLIAN MBAPPE

THE WORLD'S NO.1 WONDERKID!

MATCH tells you the story behind the teenager's rise to the top of European football!

SCHOOL OF FOOTY!

Mbappe began his footy education at the famous French academy, Clairefontaine. The school has produced tons of France stars over the years, especially strikers! The ace wonderkid is following in the footsteps of former Chelsea star Nicolas Anelka, ex-Man. United man Louis Saha and current Premier League goal king Olivier Giroud. Not much pressure, eh?

THIERRY TWO!

The footballer Mbappe shares most similarities with though, is Arsenal legend Thierry Henry. After leaving Clairefontaine, Henry signed for Monaco and became their youngest player and goalscorer – and Kylian did exactly the same! Plus, Mbappe loves drifting out to the left wing and tearing defences apart with his electric pace and finishing – just like his hero!

WANTED MAN!

Monaco's awesome run to the Champo League semi-finals caught the attention of Europe's top clubs, with Kylian scoring six times in the knockout stages. Real Madrid, Liverpool, Man. City and Arsenal were all ready to break the bank for him, but the young star chose to join PSG on loan, with an option to make the deal permanent for £165 million in 2018!

THE FUTURE?

2018 could be the year that Mbappe truly establishes himself as the world's No.1 striker! Kylian's only going to get better alongside Neymar and Edinson Cavani at PSG, and his first World Cup is just around the corner too. With this guy leading the line alongside Antoine Griezmann, France will definitely be one of the favourites at Russia 2018!

LIGUE 1 CHAMPIONS!

In 2017, the lethal France finisher took another step in Henry's footsteps by firing Monaco to the Ligue 1 title. The club topped the table and goalscoring charts for most of the season, and sealed the trophy with a 2-0 win over Saint-Etienne – with the young hitman opening the scoring. His total of 15 goals made him the top-scoring teen in Europe's top five leagues. Wow!

FACTPACK

Name: Kylian Sanmi Mbappe Lottin
Age: 18 **Position:** Forward
Club: PSG **Country:** France
Boots: Nike Hypervenom
Value: £165 million

TOP SKILLS

Skill		Rating
Dribbling		9
Pace		9
Balance		8
Finishing		8
Technique		8

TURN OVER NOW FOR MATCH'S WONDERKID TEAM!

WONDER

GIANLUIGI DONNARUMMA

Forget a wonderkid XI, Donnarumma isn't far from being the best keeper in the world, and he doesn't turn 19 until February! He's looked totally at home in Milan's net ever since making his debut as a 16-year-old, before later becoming Italy's youngest keeper too. When Gianluigi Buffon retires, The Azzurri have a ready-made replacement!

Donnarumma
AC Milan

Tuanzebe
Man. United

Tah
B. Leverkusen

Tielemans
Monaco

YOURI TIELEMANS

Tielemans was one of Europe's most in-demand wonderkids for ages before Monaco finally won the race to sign him from Anderlecht last summer. The young Belgian had caught the eye with a series of spectacular long-range goals with either foot, as he became the Belgian League's best player while still a teenager. Legend!

Asensio
Real Madrid

OUSMANE DEMBELE

French footy's the home of world-class wonderkids right now, but few of them are as good as Dembele! His rapid pace, sick tricks and close control saw Barcelona splash out £135.5 million on him as Neymar's replacement at the Nou Camp! He's so good with both feet, we're still trying to work out which side is his best!

Dembele
Barcelona

Rashford
Man. United

KID XI!

THEO HERNANDEZ

Before last summer, the Madrid clubs had an agreement not to sign each other's players, but Real broke the deal after watching Hernandez on loan at Alaves. The younger brother of Atletico CB Lucas, Theo is a pacy full-back who loves to get forward, so much so that Zinedine Zidane reckons he could replace Gareth Bale at The Bernabeu one day!

THE SUBS' BENCH

GK

Alban Lafont
Toulouse & France

Sanchez
Tottenham

Hernandez
Real Madrid

DF

Malang Sarr
Nice & France

MF

Christian Pulisic
B. Dortmund & USA

DAVINSON SANCHEZ

Sanchez was a key man in Ajax's run to the 2017 Europa League Final. He's strong and quick, and when he wins the ball back he can really play! The Colombian is hard to knock off the ball when he dribbles out from the back, and his passing is super accurate too - no wonder Tottenham paid a huge £42 million to sign him!

Alli
Tottenham

MF

Renato Sanches
Swansea & Portugal

WG

Thomas Lemar
Monaco & France

Mbappe
PSG

WG

Leroy Sane
Man. City & Germany

ST

Gabriel Jesus
Man. City & Brazil

BIG MATCH! QUIZ

PREMIER LEAGUE SPECIAL

SWITCH!

Which Premier League striker has changed careers to become a tennis player?

5 QUESTIONS ON...
ARSENAL

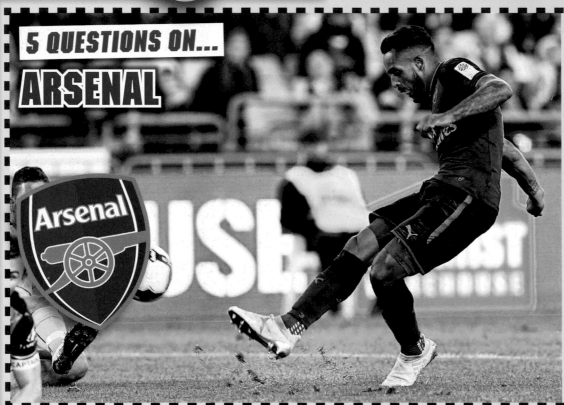

1 What is the North London club's wicked nickname - The Reds, The Gunners or The Dragons?

2 How many FA Cups have the Premier League giants won - 11, 12, 13, 14 or 15?

3 Which London club was founded first - Crystal Palace, Chelsea, Tottenham or Arsenal?

4 Is the capacity of Arsenal's awesome Emirates Stadium under 60,000 or over 60,000?

5 What shirt number does rapid forward Theo Walcott wear - No.7, No.10 or No.14?

CLOSE-UP!

Which Premier League stars have we zoomed in on?

1.

2.

3.

4.

SOCCER SCRABBLE

Rearrange these letters to figure out the name of a Premier League baller!

B₃ N₁ L₁ S₁ R₁
R₁ A₁ V₄ I₁
O₁ E₁
D₂

NAME THE TEAM!

HOME CHAMPIONS

1 **2** **3** **4** **5** **6** **7** **8** **9** **10**

Do you remember the Chelsea starting XI that beat Sunderland on the last day of 2016–17?

1. Winger ★ Belgium

2. Centre-back ★ Brazil

3. Centre-back ★ England

4. Goalkeeper ★ Belgium

Left Wing-Back ★ Spain
MARCOS ALONSO

5. Striker ★ Spain

6. Midfielder ★ France

7. Right Wing-Back ★ Nigeria

8. Midfielder ★ Spain

9. Centre-Back ★ Spain

10. Winger ★ Brazil

SUPER SKIPPERS!

Who are the captains of these mega clubs?

Man. City

Liverpool

Tottenham

West Ham

GOAL MACHINES!

Name the teams these lethal strikers play for!

1. Jermain Defoe

4. Saido Berahino

2. Christian Benteke

5. Dwight Gayle

3. Danny Welbeck

6. Steve Mounie

MATCH! WINNER!

Who scored the winning goal as Swansea beat West Brom 2-1 on the last day of the 2016–17 season?

ANSWERS ON PAGE 94

WICKED WORDFIT!

Fit the all-time Prem top scorers into this grid!

Adebayor
Aguero
Anelka
Beattie
Bent
Berbatov
Bergkamp
Cole
Crouch
Davies

Defoe
Drogba
Dublin
Ferdinand
Fowler
Gerrard
Giggs
Hasselbaink
Henry
Heskey

Keane
Lampard
Le Tissier
Lukaku
Owen
Phillips
Ronaldo
Rooney
Saha
Scholes

Shearer
Sheringham
Solskjaer
Torres
Van Nistelrooy
Van Persie
Viduka
Wright
Yakubu
Yorke

ANSWERS ON PAGE 94

MATCH!
THE BEST FOOTBALL MAGAZINE!

BALE

BOOTS

adidas X 17.1

STAT ATTACK

No British player has scored more goals in La Liga history than the lightning-fast forward!

TRANSFER VALUE

£90 MILLION

InstaMATCH!

 mbatshuayi

 1m+ followers

The Chelsea and Belgium superstar took loads of mad pics while on holiday in LA, including this snap with Kong!

 cristiano

110m+ followers

Ronaldo's such a show-off! Not only is he one of the best footballers of all time, but he drives flashy motors like this!

alexis_officia1

 7m+ followers

Sanchez used Snapchat's cool dog filter to take this barking mad selfie!

delealli36

2m+ followers

Wind-up merchant Dele Alli papped best mate Eric Dier washing the dishes!

 aubameyang97

5m+ followers

We don't know who looks more starstruck – Mickey Mouse or Aubameyang!

antogriezmann

Griezmann tagged France team-mate Paul Pogba in this Snapchat filter selfie!

12m+ followers

karimbenzema

Is this the lethal Real Madrid hitman's best hat-trick of all time?

20m+ followers

m10_official

Germany legend Mesut Ozil proves he's Arsenal through and through!

13m+ followers

iamjermaindefoe

The Bournemouth hero's right uppercut is almost as lethal as his right foot!

400k+ followers

leomessi

The shirts Barça legend Lionel Messi has collected over the years are absolutely mind-blowing! Suarez, Aguero, Di Maria, Totti, Raul, Lahm, Alves, Fabregas... the list goes on and on!

80m+ followers

iamdanielsturridge

The Liverpool striker got backstage access to one of Drake's epic gigs!

3m+ followers

2018'S A BIG YEAR FOR...
MESSI

THE STORY SO FAR...

Messi made his Barça debut in 2004, and played his first game for Argentina just a year later. Since then he's become the star for club and country, broke tons of records for both, and firmly established himself as one of the game's all-time greats!

With four Champions Leagues, eight La Ligas and tons more trophies, Leo's won the lot at Barcelona! However, last season Real Madrid claimed both crowns, inspired by Messi's great rival Cristiano Ronaldo. This year, he wants them back!

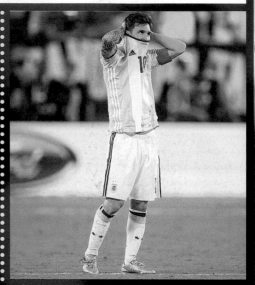

For Argentina, Messi's had a lot less luck. Since a gold medal in the 2008 Olympics, the legendary forward's been on the losing side in four finals - including two penalty shootouts! This summer's World Cup could be his last chance to win a major comp!

LEO'S WORLD CUP BID

Messi's Argentina are aiming for a fourth major final in a row in Russia after reaching three in three years recently. Germany beat them in extra-time at the 2014 World Cup, before they lost on penalties to Chile in two Copa America finals. Messi even retired after the 2016 disappointment, but then changed his mind. Good decision, mate!

INTERNATIONAL HERO

As an epic dribbler with a wicked left foot, Leo's been compared to Argentina legend Diego Maradona ever since he burst onto the scene! The Barça star has never matched his hero's achievement of inspiring his country to a tournament win, though - Maradona did in the 1986 World Cup! Messi needs to lift the trophy in Russia to become equal!

BARÇA BACK ON TOP

Before the World Cup kicks off, there's loads to sort out in Spain. Real's La Liga win ended Barcelona's run of two titles in a row, while their Champions League triumph made them the kings of Europe once again! Leo's got used to Barça being the No.1 team in Spain, but to get back on top, he'll need to take back those two trophies!

BALLON D'OR BATTLE

If the football superstar does manage to reclaim those titles, he'll be the massive favourite for the next Ballon d'Or! The Barcelona magician is constantly battling Ronaldo for footy's top individual award, and winning it again this year would go a long way to settling the debate on who's better out of the two footy megastars!

2018 IN NUMBERS...

5 — A fifth CL title would make Messi the most successful non-European in the comp's history!

8 — The 2018 World Cup will be Lionel's eighth senior international tournament!

10 — If he scores five times in Russia, he'll go level with Gabriel Batistuta's Argentina record of ten WC goals!

400 — This year, Leo should play in his 400th La Liga match!

ULTIMATE GUIDE TO THE...
WORLD CUP!

FIFA WORLD CUP
RUSSIA 2018

Russia 2018 kicks off this summer, so MATCH tells you everything you need to know about the epic tournament!

4 FAMOUS TROPHY

The World Cup trophy is without doubt the most famous and recognisable trophy in world football! It's made of 18 karat gold, weighs just over 6kg and shows two human figures holding up the Earth!

1 THE HOSTS

Russia 2018 will be the first time ever that Eastern Europe has hosted the World Cup, and only once - when Spain staged World Cup 1982 with 17 venues - has there been more stadiums at a final tournament in one country!

2 QUALIFYING RECORD

All 210 official FIFA member nations entered qualifying, the largest number of all time, although Zimbabwe and Indonesia were later disqualified. Bhutan, South Sudan, Gibraltar and Kosovo made their WC quali debuts!

3 SAMBA STARS

Other than the host nation Russia, Brazil became the first country to qualify for the tournament after hammering Paraguay 3-0 in March 2017, thanks to goals by Philippe Coutinho, Neymar and Marcelo!

6 MEGA MASCOT

A wolf called Zabivaka, which means 'The one who scores' in Russian, is the 2018 World Cup's official mascot. He was picked by the public after one million people voted back in September 2016!

7 GOAL MACHINES

The World Cup always unearths goal kings! The 2014 edition saw Colombia hero James Rodriguez win the Golden Boot, all-time World Cup top goalscorer Miroslav Klose bagged the 2006 award and no-one will forget Toto Schillaci's awesome breakthrough at Italia '90!

8 MOST APPS

Italy's Gianluigi Buffon is one of only three players, along with Lothar Matthaus and Antonio Carbajal, to be picked by his country for five different World Cups! He'll make that six and hold the record outright if he's picked for Russia 2018!

9 BONKERS STATS

More than 1 billion supporters watched the 2014 World Cup Final! The tournament itself attracted a TV audience of 3.2 billion and an online audience of 280 million – and those numbers are expected to rise for 2018!

5 THE HOLDERS

After winning their fourth World Cup at Brazil 2014, Germany will be aiming to retain their crown at Russia 2018 and join the Samba Stars on five WC victories! We wouldn't bet against it happening, either!

10 VIDEO ASSISTANT REFS

Russia 2018 could see VARs being used for the first time ever at a World Cup! The video technology system was trialled at the 2017 Confederations Cup, and officials will decide in March if it'll be used at the World Cup!

Now turn over for our World Cup 2018 Stadium Guide!

WORLD CUP 2018...
STADIUM GUIDE!

MATCH takes a closer look at all of Russia 2018's host stadiums!

VOLGOGRAD ARENA

City: Volgograd
Capacity: 45,568

This was built on the site of the Central Stadium, home to Rotor Volgograd, who knocked Man. United out of Europe in 1995! The roof's built with cables that look like bicycle wheel spokes!

SAINT PETERSBURG STADIUM

City: Saint Petersburg ★ **Capacity:** 68,134

The second-biggest ground at Russia 2018 enjoyed a decent dress rehearsal in 2017 by hosting the Confederations Cup final. The mind-blowing arena has a retractable roof and a sliding pitch!

FISHT STADIUM

City: Sochi
Capacity: 47,700

This stadium is located in the Olympic Park that hosted the 2014 Winter Olympics. Its silhouette resembles a snow-capped mountain peak in the Caucasus range!

SAMARA ARENA

City: Samara
Capacity: 44,807

Work began on this in 2014, and it's estimated it'll cost around £250 million to complete! After the World Cup, Krylia Sovetov Samara's awesome new home will be called the Cosmos Arena!

KAZAN ARENA

City: Kazan
Capacity: 44,779

Kazan Arena was designed by the same architects behind Wembley and Arsenal's Emirates. From the sky it looks like a water lily, plus it has the largest outside screen in Europe!

KALININGRAD STADIUM

City: Kaliningrad
Capacity: 35,212

This new ground is the smallest of all the venues at Russia 2018. Kaliningrad also isn't actually connected to Russia's mainland – the city is landlocked between Poland and Lithuania!

SPARTAK STADIUM

City: Moscow
Capacity: 43,298

This venue is home to one of Russia's most famous clubs - Spartak Moscow. The diamonds on the outside of the stadium represent the club's flag, plus they can change colour too!

LUZHNIKI STADIUM

City: Moscow
Capacity: 81,006

The iconic Luzhniki Stadium will host the tournament's opening game and the World Cup final. It's the biggest of all Russia 2018's grounds and hosted the 2008 Champions League Final!

NIZHNY NOVGOROD STADIUM

City: Nizhny Novgorod ★ **Capacity:** 45,331

This is another of Russia 2018's new stadiums, and it's built at the junction of the Volga and Oka rivers. Its home team, Olympiets Nizhny Novgorod, play in the second tier of Russian football!

EKATERINBURG ARENA

City: Ekaterinburg ★ **Capacity:** 35,696

The original stadium was built in 1953 and is home to one of Russia oldest clubs, FC Ural. A roof and temporary stand will be installed in time for the World Cup to help increase its total capacity!

MORDOVIA ARENA

City: Saransk
Capacity: 44,442

Named after the Republic of Mordovia, work to build this venue began in 2010. It's shaped like an oval, and its orange, red and white colours represent Mordovia's arts and crafts!

ROSTOV ARENA

City: Rostov-on-Don
Capacity: 45,145

The jaw-dropping new Rostov Arena replaces Olimp-2 as FC Rostov's home stadium. During its construction in 2014, five shells from World War II were discovered!

WIN THE WORLD CUP!

Go all the way from the playground to the World Cup final! Use some coins as counters, grab a dice and battle loads of your mates in this epic footy board game!

37 LEGEND! You hit a hat-trick in the World Cup semi-final! Move forward three spaces!

38

39 FAIL! You pick up a serious knee injury in the World Cup semi-final. Move back six spaces!

40

41 FAIL! You miss an absolute sitter in the World Cup final! Move back five spaces!

WINNER! YOU'RE A FOOTY LEGEND! YOU'VE WON THE WORLD CUP!

36

35 LEGEND! You're named in your country's squad for the World Cup! Move forward one space!

34 FAIL! You don't get picked in your country's final World Cup squad. Move back three spaces!

33

32 FAIL! You pick up a hamstring injury just before the World Cup. Move back four spaces!

31

25 FAIL! You're sent off against your team's local rivals! Move back three spaces!

26

27 LEGEND! You help your team win the Premier league title! Move forward four spaces!

28

29 FAIL! Your Premier League team gets relegated and you get sold! Move back six spaces!

30 LEGEND! You score the winner in the Champions League final! Move forward three spaces!

24 LEGEND! A top-four Premier League club spends £10 million on you! Move forward two spaces!

23

22

21 LEGEND! You have an epic interview and massive poster in MATCH! Move forward two spaces!

20 FAIL! You hand in a transfer request after getting your head turned. Move back one space!

19

13

14 LEGEND! A big Championship club signs you up! Move forward two spaces!

15 FAIL! The fans are annoyed after you say you want a move to the Prem. Move back two spaces!

16

17 FAIL! You scuff a penalty in the play-off semi-final. Move back four spaces!

18 LEGEND! You score a last-minute winner in the play-off final! Move forward four spaces!

12 FAIL! Your manager fines you a week's wages for a Twitter gaffe! Move back three spaces!

11

10 FAIL! You miss a last-minute penalty in the Carabao Cup. Move back one space!

9

8 LEGEND! A League One team signs you up after a top run of form! Move forward three spaces!

7

START KICK-OFF! The player who rolls the highest number goes first!

2

3 FAIL! A scout comes to watch you play, but you have a total shocker! Move back a space!

4

5 LEGEND! A League Two side offers you a contract after a great trial! Move forward two spaces!

6

MATCH!
THE BEST FOOTBALL MAGAZINE!

POGBA

adidas

CHEVROLET

FAB FACT
The Man. United and France midfield machine was the first Prem footballer to get his own Twitter Emoji!

BOOTS
adidas ACE 17+

STAT ATTACK
The £89 million man hit more through balls than any other player in the Premier League last season. He's a pass master!

TRANSFER VALUE

£90 MILLION

IF FOOTY STARS WERE... EMOJIS!

Whether it's a tongue out or hiding monkey, MATCH loves seeing footy heroes pulling funny faces like Emojis. Check them out!

NEY PRAY

NEYMAR
PSG

MOU'S SMOOCH

PUCKER UP!

JOSE MOURINHO
Man. United

BLOW-UP BANANA

PREFER APPLES MYSELF!

JOEL ROBLES
Everton

GRUMPY RON

WHO NICKED MY HAIR GEL?

CRISTIANO RONALDO
Real Madrid

HART ACHE

I'M SEEING STARS!

JOE HART
West Ham

HI-FIVE

DON'T LEAVE ME HANGING!

ARJEN ROBBEN
Bayern Munich

MATCH! 33

BIG MATCH! QUIZ

WORLD CUP SPECIAL

Holland	England	Uruguay	Argentina

ODD ONE OUT!
Which of these countries has never won the World Cup?

Spain

Brazil

FLIPPED!
Which Portugal hero has had his face messed up in this weird pic?

CRAZY KIT!
Which country wore this eye-buster in 2018 WC qualifying?

MEGA MASH-UP!

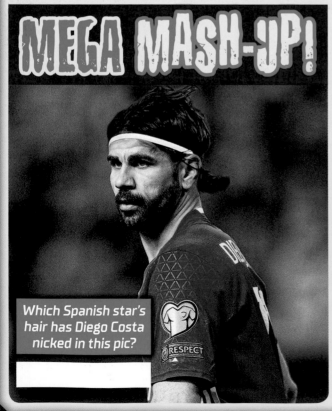

Which Spanish star's hair has Diego Costa nicked in this pic?

STADIUM GAME
Match these stadiums to the 2018 WC teams who play there!

Estadio Azteca	Stade de France	Estadio Nacional	Wembley
1	2	3	4

A	B	C	D
England	France	Mexico	Chile

SPOT THE BALL!

Mark where you think the ball is in this 2018 WC qualifying pic!

A B C D E F G H I J K

1 2 3 4 5 6 7 8 9 10 11 12 13 14 15 16 17 18 19

2010

2006

GUESS THE WINNERS!

Do you know which countries won these World Cups?

2002

1998

World Cup Stoppers!

Name the countries these GKs played for!

1. Jens Lehmann

2. Paul Robinson

3. Andreas Isaksson

4. Shaka Hislop

5. Edwin van der Sar

6. Ricardo

MATCH! WINNER!

Can you remember who scored the only goal in Germany's 2014 World Cup Final win against Argentina?

ANSWERS ON PAGE 94

MEGA WORDSEARCH

Can you find the legendary World Cup heroes in this giant grid?

Baggio	Brehme	Charlton	Fontaine	Klose	Maldini	Pele	Schillaci
Banks	Buffon	Cubillas	Hurst	Kocsis	Maradona	Rahn	Seeler
Batistuta	Cafu	Djalma Santos	Jairzinho	Lahm	Matthaus	Rivaldo	Thuram
Beckenbauer	Cannavaro	Dunga	Kempes	Lato	Moore	Ronaldo	Zidane
Boniek	Carbajal	Eusebio	Klinsmann	Lineker	Muller	Rossi	Zoff

ANSWERS ON PAGE 94

2018'S A BIG YEAR FOR...
ROONEY

Can Wazza get back to the top of his game?

THE STORY SO FAR...

In 2002, Rooney burst onto the scene by becoming the Prem's youngest ever scorer with a screamer against Arsenal. An awesome Euro 2004 for England earned him a mega move to Man. United, which made Roo the most expensive teenager ever!

Over 13 years at Old Trafford, Wazza won five league titles and the Champions League, along with tons of other major trophies! He sealed his status as a Red Devils legend in January 2017, by becoming the club's all-time record goalscorer!

After falling down the pecking order at Old Trafford, Rooney returned to his boyhood club Everton on a free transfer. The goal king is fully focused on firing The Toffees into Europe again after retiring from international football in August!

HOMEGROWN HERO

Everton's academy has produced some great talent over the years, but none have been as successful as Rooney. With The Toffees' next generation of wonderkids coming through to the first team, he'll play a big role in developing their young stars, plus he could help ensure the next Evertonian star is a success at Goodison Park, not Old Trafford!

TOP-FOUR ATTEMPT

Only three teams have won the league more times than Everton, but Roo was only a baby last time they lifted the title in 1987 – and he's never seen them play in the Champions League. This year he wants that to change by helping the Merseyside club become title challengers once again, and give them a taste of top European footy!

EUROPA LEAGUE

With over 100 games in the Europa and Champions League, Rooney is Everton's most experienced player in European football by far! The lethal finsher will play a massive part in The Toffees' Euro campaign in 2017-18, and he'll be desperate to lift the Europa League trophy again – just like he did in his last game for Man. United in 2016-17!

PREM LEGEND

People forget Rooney is already the Premier League's second top goalscorer in history! Alan Shearer is still out in front on 260, but if Wazza can close the gap this year, he'll believe that he can overtake the Newcastle legend before he retires, and establish himself as the greatest goalscorer England's top division has ever had!

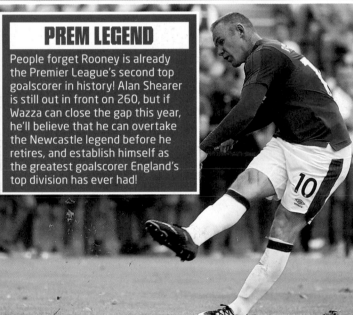

2018 IN NUMBERS...

16
In August, it'll be 16 years since Rooney made his Prem debut against Tottenham!

50
Roo could become the first Englishman to reach 50 goals in European club footy!

17
The Everton star's next major trophy will be the 17th of his career!

100
He could reach 100 Everton appearances in all competitions this year!

Everton
1878
NIL SATIS NISI OPTIMUM

ALL-TIME
PREMIER LEAGUE DREAM TEAM!

Pick your team of the Prem's best ever players, and if it's the same as MATCH's you could win an awesome prize!

PREM DREAM TEAM
GOALKEEPERS!

PETER SCHMEICHEL

Main Club: Man. United

With more league titles than any other goalkeeper, Schmeichel is the Prem's most successful stopper ever. The big Dane played for United when they won the treble in 1999, and was the first GK to score a goal in the Prem after he joined Aston Villa!

PETR CECH

Main Clubs: Arsenal & Chelsea

Cech's one of the Prem's most iconic keepers – and not just because of his trademark headgear! Not only has he kept more clean sheets than any GK in the league's history, he was also in net for Chelsea when they conceded the fewest goals in a season ever!

THIBAUT COURTOIS

Main Club: Chelsea

Only a special keeper could replace Petr Cech at Chelsea, and that's what Courtois is! The Belgian spent three years on loan at Atletico Madrid after joining The Blues, and since returning to Stamford Bridge, he's become one of the best goalkeepers in Europe!

HUGO LLORIS

Main Club: Tottenham

The sweeper-keeper's ability to rush out of his box and clean up opposition attacks has been one of the keys to Tottenham's rise to the top in recent years. Lloris' legendary leadership skills have also seen him become skipper of both Spurs and France!

PEPE REINA

Main Club: Liverpool

Rafa Benitez said he'd signed 'the best keeper in Spain' when Reina moved to Liverpool in 2005, and he quickly became one of the best in England too! After joining, the ex-Barcelona man won the Premier League Golden Glove award three years in a row!

BEST OF THE REST!
CHECK OUT THESE OTHER SUPERSTARS!

EDWIN VAN DER SAR
Main Clubs: Man. United & Fulham

DAVID JAMES
Main Clubs: Liverpool & Portsmouth

DAVID SEAMAN
Main Club: Arsenal

DAVID DE GEA
Main Club: Man. United

NOW PICK YOUR ALL-TIME PREM DREAM TEAM GOALKEEPER! TURN TO PAGE 52

PREM DREAM TEAM
CENTRE-BACKS!

DAVID LUIZ

Main Club: Chelsea

Luiz wouldn't have got near this list after his first spell at Chelsea, but his role in their title-winning season of 2016-17 proved how good he is! Not only is he a top-class CB, but he's also got the passing and dribbling ability to be a playmaker from the back!

VINCENT KOMPANY

Main Club: Man. City

City fans must wonder how much more they could have won if Kompany had stayed fit! Their skipper has played a big part in the club's success as both an inspirational leader and a world-class defender, and was named the Prem Player Of The Year in 2011-12!

JAAP STAM

Main Club: Man. United

Legendary boss Alex Ferguson didn't make many mistakes, but one decision he does regret is selling Stam! The Dutchman was the complete defender with pace, strength and top tackling. If he'd stayed at Old Trafford, he'd have defo added to his three titles!

TONY ADAMS

Main Club: Arsenal

Adams was known for his leadership at the back, but his most famous moment came in the other penalty area! In Arsenal's title-deciding fixture of 1997-98, he strode out from the back and lashed the ball home to seal Arsene Wenger's first Prem title!

LEDLEY KING

Main Club: Tottenham

If it hadn't been for injury, King would have doubled his 268 Prem games and tripled his 21 England caps! The quick centre-back remained a regular for Spurs right up until the end of his career, even though he was unable to train because of knee problems!

BEST OF THE REST!
CHECK OUT THESE OTHER SUPERSTARS!

NEMANJA VIDIC
Main Club:
Man. United

SYLVAIN DISTIN
Main Clubs:
Everton & Man. City

SAMI HYYPIA
Main Club:
Liverpool

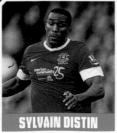

MARTIN KEOWN
Main Club:
Arsenal

RICARDO CARVALHO
Main Club:
Chelsea

JOHN TERRY

Main Club: Chelsea

Captain, leader, legend – those were the words on a flag at Stamford Bridge until JT moved to Aston Villa, and they summed him up perfectly! He was at the heart of The Blues' success over the past 17 years, and nobody's won more Prem titles as skipper than him!

RIO FERDINAND

Main Clubs: Man. United & West Ham

At his peak, Rio was Europe's best CB – he broke the transfer record for a British player and a defender twice! His mega £18m move from West Ham to Leeds took him from a young talent to a CL defender, and his £30m switch to Man. United made him a world star!

JAMIE CARRAGHER

Main Club: Liverpool

Although Carragher was never blessed with bags of pace or loads of natural talent, his on-pitch intelligence and determination to win made him a class defender. Nobody's played more Prem games for the club than Carra, making him an all-time Reds legend!

GARETH SOUTHGATE

Main Clubs: Aston Villa & Boro

The England boss began his career at Crystal Palace as a midfielder, but switched to CB after joining Aston Villa in 1995. He skippered Middlesbrough to their League Cup success in 2004, captained all of the clubs he played for and won 57 international caps!

SOL CAMPBELL

Main Clubs: Arsenal & Tottenham

Campbell's move between the North London clubs in 2001 is still one of the most controversial transfer ever! The powerhouse was one of Europe's top centre-backs at the time, and went on to win two titles for Arsenal, playing a key role in their invincible season!

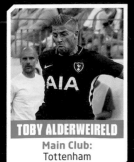

TOBY ALDERWEIRELD
Main Club:
Tottenham

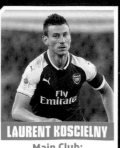

LAURENT KOSCIELNY
Main Club:
Arsenal

GARY CAHILL
Main Clubs:
Chelsea & Bolton

JOHN STONES
Main Clubs:
Man. City & Everton

JAN VERTONGHEN
Main Club:
Tottenham

NOW PICK YOUR ALL-TIME PREM DREAM TEAM CENTRE-BACKS!

TURN TO PAGE 52

PREM DREAM TEAM
FULL-BACKS!

GARY NEVILLE

Main Club: Man. United

Before he became a top footy pundit, G-Nev was one of the most consistent right-backs in the country! Alongside The Red Devils' other academy stars, the local lad won everything in his 602 appearances for United, and not many left wingers got the better of him!

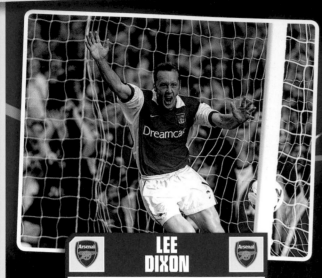

LEE DIXON

Main Club: Arsenal

Dixon played in one of the most solid and well-drilled back fours ever alongside Tony Adams, Steve Bould and Nigel Winterburn! The right-back was a quality crosser that loved to get forward, and ended his career with two Premier League titles!

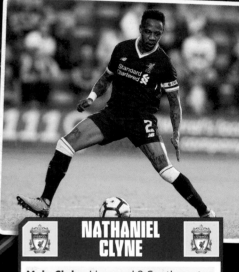

PABLO ZABALETA

Main Clubs: West Ham & Man. City

Zaba arrived in Manchester the same week as City's billionaire owners, and he went on to become a big fans' fave! His rock-solid displays and determined attitude made him one of the club's most important players – and now he wants to do the same at West Ham!

KYLE WALKER

Main Clubs: Man. City & Tottenham

The Prem's quickest defender became its most expensive when he joined Man. City from Tottenham in 2017. Walker's electric speed doesn't just make him a great attacking option from full-back, it also means that no winger in the world can beat him for pace!

NATHANIEL CLYNE

Main Clubs: Liverpool & Southampton

Clyne is competing with Walker for the title of the Prem's current best RB, and for the England No.2 shirt too! Although the ex-Crystal Palace and Southampton man has often come second, his best is yet to come, and on his day he's as good as anybody!

BEST OF THE REST!

CHECK OUT THESE OTHER SUPERSTARS!

BRANISLAV IVANOVIC
Main Club: Chelsea

LAUREN
Main Club: Arsenal

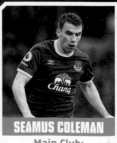

SEAMUS COLEMAN
Main Club: Everton

CESAR AZPILICUETA
Main Club: Chelsea

HECTOR BELLERIN
Main Club: Arsenal

LEIGHTON BAINES

Main Clubs: Everton & Wigan

Plenty of full-backs are able to fly forward to support attacks, but not many have the quality of delivery that Baines does! His crossing from set-pieces and open play is world class, and in 2017 he bagged his 50th Prem assist – a record for a defender!

DANNY ROSE

Main Club: Tottenham

Rose burst onto the scene at Spurs in the most spectacular way possible – with a 30-yard thunderbolt on his debut in the North London derby! Since then, he's been converted from a left winger into one of the quickest and most consistent LBs in the Prem!

ASHLEY COLE

Main Clubs: Chelsea & Arsenal

One of the best LBs ever regularly dominated the Prem's best wingers, including Cristiano Ronaldo more than once! England's most-capped full-back ever played a huge part in Arsenal's invincible season, before going on to win another title at Chelsea!

IAN HARTE

Main Club: Leeds

Harte was a superstar in the Leeds side that challenged at the top of the Prem in the late 90s and reached the Champions League semis in 2000-01. His energy from left-back was key to their success, as were his lethal free-kicks and long-range shots!

STUART PEARCE

Main Club: Nottingham Forest

With a fierce left foot and an even fiercer tackle, 'Psycho' was one of the toughest players in the history of English football! His penalties and free-kicks were unstoppable, and he could mark opponents out of a game through pure fear!

GRAEME LE SAUX
Main Clubs:
Chelsea & Blackburn

DENIS IRWIN
Main Club:
Man. United

JOHN ARNE RIISE
Main Clubs:
Liverpool & Fulham

RYAN BERTRAND
Main Clubs:
Southampton & Chelsea

PATRICE EVRA
Main Club:
Man. United

NOW PICK YOUR ALL-TIME PREM DREAM TEAM FULLS-BACKS!

TURN TO PAGE 52

PREM DREAM TEAM
MIDFIELDERS!

STEVEN GERRARD

Main Club: Liverpool

Liverpool could always turn to club legend Stevie G for a goal or moment of magic, and he inspired countless comebacks! He was at the heart of their closest title challenges – first as a goalscoring CAM in 2008-09, then as a dominant holding CM in 2013-14!

N'GOLO KANTE

Main Clubs: Chelsea & Leicester

Not many players have had as big an impact on the Prem as lung-buster Kante! The France midfielder was the heartbeat of the Leicester team that shocked the world by winning the title in 2015-16, before moving to Chelsea and doing the same thing again!

FRANK LAMPARD

Main Club: Chelsea

The Prem's highest-scoring midfielder ever started at West Ham, but became a legend at Chelsea. Lamps timed his runs into the box perfectly to get on the end of chances, and his long-range shooting meant he regularly went close to 20 Prem goals a season!

GARY SPEED

Main Clubs: Newcastle & Leeds

Only four players have played more Premier League games than the Wales legend! Speed's consistency and incredible fitness allowed him to play 535 times in the Prem, while his sweet left foot and bullet headers made him a key man for all his clubs!

JAY-JAY OKOCHA

Main Club: Bolton

One of the most entertaining players in Prem history joined Bolton after the 2002 World Cup, and he lit up The Reebok with brilliant trickery and flair! His epic stepovers, rainbow flicks and rocket free-kicks helped keep The Trotters up season after season!

BEST OF THE REST!
CHECK OUT THESE OTHER SUPERSTARS!

CLAUDE MAKELELE
Main Club:
Chelsea

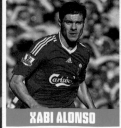

XABI ALONSO
Main Club:
Liverpool

LUKA MODRIC
Main Club:
Tottenham

ADAM LALLANA
Main Clubs:
Liverpool & Southampton

MICHAEL CARRICK
Main Clubs:
Man. United & West Ham

DELE ALLI

Main Club: Tottenham

Alli's only played two full Premier League seasons, but he's already a megastar! His natural instinct is to get into dangerous positions, plus his top-class finishing skills mean he's evolved from an all-action central midfielder to a goal-poaching No.10!

PAUL SCHOLES

Main Club: Man. United

Possibly the best passer in Premier League history, Scholes started out as a box-to-box goalscoring midfielder but turned into a deep-lying creator as he got older. Legends of the game Zinedine Zidane and Xavi both claim he was the best midfielder in Europe!

ROY KEANE

Main Club: Man. United

Skipper Keane was at the heart of United's dominant team of the 90s. He could grab games by the scruff of the neck with a driving run, a crunching challenge or a defence-splitting pass, and his presence on the pitch inspired team-mates and terrified opponents!

PATRICK VIEIRA

Main Club: Arsenal

One of Arsene Wenger's first signings at Arsenal became his midfield general for almost ten years. Vieira could do everything - his passing, tackling and dribbling, combined with his strength and energy, meant he powered his team on to three Prem titles!

YAYA TOURE

Main Club: Man. City

Yaya won games on his own at his peak for City! He made his name as a DM at Barcelona, but developed into a dominant box-to-box player in the Prem, with the technical ability to pass and dribble like a star, and the physicality to dominate opponents!

MESUT OZIL
Main Club:
Arsenal

CESC FABREGAS
Main Clubs:
Chelsea & Arsenal

JUAN MATA
Main Clubs:
Man. United & Chelsea

MICHAEL ESSIEN
Main Club:
Chelsea

PAUL POGBA
Main Club:
Man. United

NOW PICK YOUR ALL-TIME PREM DREAM TEAM MIDFIELDERS!

TURN TO PAGE 52

PREM DREAM TEAM
WINGERS!

 CRISTIANO RONALDO

Main Club: Man. United

Ronaldo had big shoes to fill when he inherited Man. United's No.7 shirt from David Beckham, but the Portugal hero surpassed the England legend! Not many players have dominated the Premier League in the way CR7 did from 2006 to 2009!

 EDEN HAZARD

Main Club: Chelsea

Hazard was one of the most-wanted players in Europe when he joined Chelsea for £32m in 2012, and he's proven why ever since! The Belgian played a huge role in The Blues' last two Prem title wins with dazzling dribbling and class creativity!

RIYAD MAHREZ

Main Club: Leicester

Mahrez will go down in history as one of Leicester's all-time greats after his role in The Foxes' historic title win! The winger picked up the PFA Player Of The Year award after bagging 17 goals and 11 assists, and he's still one of Europe's best dribblers!

DAVID GINOLA

Main Clubs: Spurs & Newcastle

Ginola's arrival at Newcastle in 1995 helped turn Kevin Keegan's side into one of the most entertaining teams around! The graceful but powerful dribbler was unstoppable as The Magpies almost won the league, before going on to shine at Tottenham too!

 PHILIPPE COUTINHO

Main Club: Liverpool

Signing Coutinho for £8.5 million in 2013 has turned out to be one of The Reds' best Prem bargains! The Brazil wizard has bagged double figures for goals and assists combined in every full season at Anfield, and wins games all on his own with moments of magic!

BEST OF THE REST!
CHECK OUT THESE OTHER SUPERSTARS!

DAMIEN DUFF

Main Clubs: Blackburn, Chelsea & Fulham

CHRISTIAN ERIKSEN

Main Club: Tottenham

SADIO MANE

Main Clubs: Liverpool & Southampton

MARC OVERMARS

Main Club: Arsenal

DAVID BECKHAM

Main Club: Man. United

RYAN GIGGS

Main Club: Man. United

With more title wins, assists and appearances than any other player, Giggs is the most successful player in Prem history! At his peak, the Welsh wizard was as quick as an Olympic sprinter, and turned defenders inside out with his mazy dribbling skills!

GARETH BALE

Main Club: Tottenham

Bale's career probably had a bigger turnaround than any other Premier League player! As Spurs' reserve LB, he waited 24 games before he won his first game, but after that moved up the pitch to become one of the most devastating wingers ever!

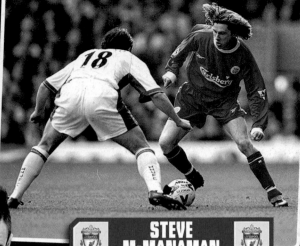

STEVE McMANAMAN

Main Club: Liverpool

Local lad McManaman was a hero at Anfield after emerging from the academy at the birth of the Premier League. His intelligence and dribbling made him an assist machine for The Reds, and he went on to win the Champo League at Real Madrid too!

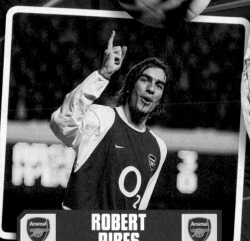

ROBERT PIRES

Main Club: Arsenal

Plenty of wingers had more pace than Pires, but not many had his intelligence, flair or ability to score wondergoals! His Arsenal career was littered with darting runs from the left wing on to his right foot, followed by delicate chips or curling top-corner screamers!

DAVID SILVA

Main Club: Man. City

Although he often starts matches in wide positions, Silva does his best work when moving into central areas. With impeccable ball control and class creativity, the Spaniard has proven that smaller players can play in the Prem and boss games too!

JOE COLE
Main Clubs:
Chelsea & West Ham

KEVIN DE BRUYNE
Main Club:
Man. City

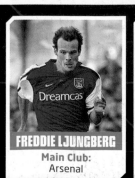

FREDDIE LJUNGBERG
Main Club:
Arsenal

ARJEN ROBBEN
Main Club:
Chelsea

ALEXIS SANCHEZ
Main Club:
Arsenal

NOW PICK YOUR ALL-TIME PREM DREAM TEAM WINGERS!

TURN TO PAGE 52

PREM DREAM TEAM
STRIKERS!

THIERRY HENRY
Main Club: Arsenal

Henry's net-busters fired The Gunners to two Premier League titles, three FA Cups and their only Champions League final. He also collected four Prem Golden Boots along the way, and became the league's all-time top-scoring foreign player. Legend!

ANDY COLE
Main Clubs: Man. United & Newcastle

Only two players have scored more Prem goals than Cole, who was lethal for Newcastle, Man. United, Blackburn and Fulham. His tally of 34 goals in 1993-94 remains a league record, and he was also the first player to score five times in one match!

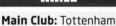

MICHAEL OWEN
Main Club: Liverpool

Within a year of bursting onto the scene as a 17-year-old in 1997, Owen had bagged a Prem Golden Boot and become an England regular! His goals in 2000-01 sealed a treble of trophies for Liverpool, and made him the last English player to win the Ballon d'Or!

HARRY KANE
Main Club: Tottenham

After a few uninspiring loan spells, some footy experts wondered if Kane was cut out for the top level, but he's proved them wrong big-time! After smashing 20+ goals three seasons in a row, the England striker has his eye on the Prem's all-time scoring record!

DIDIER DROGBA
Main Club: Chelsea

After joining for £24m in 2004, Drog became one of Chelsea's best signings of the Roman Abramovich era! Not only did he score 100 league goals in his first spell – including 29 in the title winning season of 2009-10 – his pace and power made him unplayable!

BEST OF THE REST!
CHECK OUT THESE OTHER SUPERSTARS!

RUUD VAN NISTELROOY
Main Club:
Man. United

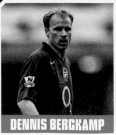

TEDDY SHERINGHAM
Main Clubs:
Spurs & Man. United

DENNIS BERGKAMP
Main Club:
Arsenal

GIANFRANCO ZOLA
Main Club:
Chelsea

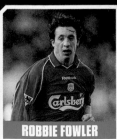

ROBBIE FOWLER
Main Club:
Liverpool

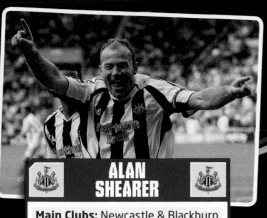

ALAN SHEARER

Main Clubs: Newcastle & Blackburn

The Prem's all-time top scorer made his name at Blackburn by winning the title in a deadly partnership with Chris Sutton known as the SAS! He then joined Newcastle for a world-record fee, and became his hometown club's all-time top scorer too!

SERGIO AGUERO

Main Club: Man. City

Aguero has scored over 120 league goals for Man. City, but he'd be a legend at the club if he'd only ever scored one! His late winner against QPR in their title-deciding match of 2011-12 was one of the most dramatic Prem moments ever!

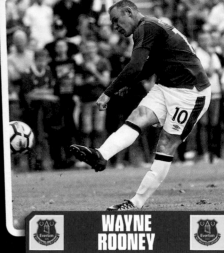

WAYNE ROONEY

Main Club: Everton & Man. United

'Remember the name, Wayne Rooney' screamed the commentator after the 16-year-old's first Prem goal – a screamer against Arsenal. Since then, Wazza has had a truly unforgettable career, becoming Man. United and England's all-time top goalscorer!

JERMAIN DEFOE

Main Clubs: Bournemouth & Spurs

JD's been one of the most consistent Prem scorers ever since his West Ham debut in 2000! The England striker has scored goals at every club he's been at, even relegated Sunderland, and is widely regarded as one of the best finishers the country's produced!

LUIS SUAREZ

Main Club: Liverpool

The closest Liverpool have come to the title was with Luis up front in 2013-14. The Uruguayan was unstoppable – not only did he have incredible skill and finishing ability, his work-rate set the tone for one of the most attacking and entertaining Prem teams ever!

IAN WRIGHT
Main Club:
Arsenal

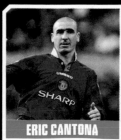

ERIC CANTONA
Main Clubs:
Man. United & Leeds

MATT LE TISSIER
Main Club:
Southampton

LES FERDINAND
Main Clubs: Spurs,
QPR & Newcastle

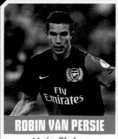

ROBIN VAN PERSIE
Main Clubs:
Arsenal & Man. United

NOW PICK YOUR ALL-TIME PREM DREAM TEAM STRIKERS!

TURN TO PAGE 52

PREM DREAM TEAM
MY ALL-TIME XI!

You've seen MATCH's all-time Prem shortlist, now pick your fave starting XI!

GOALKEEPER

RIGHT-BACK

CENTRE-BACK

CENTRE-BACK

LEFT-BACK

WINGER

MIDFIELDER

MIDFIELDER

WINGER

STRIKER

STRIKER

CAVANI

FAB FACT

Cavani's £55 million move to PSG from Napoli back in 2013 made him the most expensive transfer in Ligue 1 history!

BOOTS

Nike Hypervenom

STAT ATTACK

Edinson hit 35 Ligue 1 goals last season - only Lionel Messi bagged more in Europe's top five leagues!

£60 MILLION

DRAW YOUR OWN BOOTS!

There are tons of cool boots around right now, so why not design your own pair for the chance to win a top prize?

Name:

Date of birth:

Address:

Boot size:

Mobile:

Email:

FOOTY STARS AS KIDS

MATCH blows the dust off some ancient photo albums and raids footy stars' Instagram pages to reveal what they looked like when they were younger!

DANIEL STURRIDGE
LIVERPOOL

CHRISTIAN ERIKSEN
TOTTENHAM

PAUL POGBA
MAN. UNITED

JORDAN AYEW
SWANSEA

ALEX IWOBI
ARSENAL

ONCE A GUNNER, ALWAYS A GUNNER!

ERR... HORROR HAIR ALERT!

DAVID DE GEA
MAN. UNITED

HOW DID YOU FIND THIS, MATCH?

RAHEEM STERLING
MAN. CITY

ANGEL DI MARIA
PSG

PAST THREE LIONS LEGEND...

...FUTURE THREE LIONS LEGEND!

AARON RAMSEY
ARSENAL

HARRY KANE
TOTTENHAM

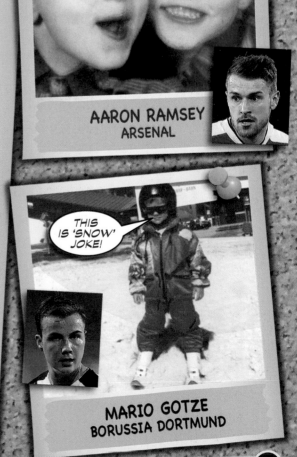

THIS IS 'SNOW' JOKE!

MARIO GOTZE
BORUSSIA DORTMUND

DID YOU GUESS IT WAS ME?

MARCUS RASHFORD
MAN. UNITED

EMRE CAN
LIVERPOOL

ANDY CARROLL
WEST HAM

JORDON IBE
BOURNEMOUTH

SEE, I ALWAYS LOVED NET!

CRISTIANO RONALDO
REAL MADRID

KARATE KID IN THE HOUSE!

DAVID LUIZ
CHELSEA

LUKE SHAW
MAN. UNITED

OZIL LOVES A DUMMY!

MESUT OZIL
ARSENAL

NEYMAR
PSG

FERNANDO TORRES
ATLETICO MADRID

GARY CAHILL
CHELSEA

JESSE LINGARD
MAN. UNITED

ALEXIS SANCHEZ
ARSENAL

JORDAN HENDERSON
LIVERPOOL

CHRIS SMALLING
MAN. UNITED

PREMIER LEAGUE

Get a load of the
Prem's top scorers
from countries all
around the world!

NORTH AMERICA

Player/Country	Goals
Dwight Yorke *Trinidad & Tobago*	123
Clint Dempsey *United States*	57
Jason Euell *Jamaica*	56
Paulo Wanchope *Costa Rica*	50
Javier Hernandez *Mexico*	37
Ruel Fox *Montserrat*	36
Jason Roberts *Grenada*	36
Tomasz Radzinski *Canada*	35
Carl Cort *Guyana*	28
Shaun Goater *Bermuda*	13
Emmerson Boyce *Barbados*	11

SOUTH AMERICA

Player/Country	Goals
Sergio Aguero *Argentina*	122
Luis Suarez *Uruguay*	69
Alexis Sanchez *Chile*	53
Nolberto Solano *Peru*	49
Juan Pablo Angel *Colombia*	44
Philippe Coutinho *Brazil*	34
Roque Santa Cruz *Paraguay*	26
Antonio Valencia *Ecuador*	21
Salomon Rondon *Venezuela*	17

AFRICA

Player/Country	Goals
Didier Drogba *Ivory Coast*	104
Emmanuel Adebayor *Togo*	97
Yakubu *Nigeria*	95
Demba Ba *Senegal*	43
Freddie Kanoute *Mali*	43
Benni McCarthy *South Africa*	37
Peter Ndlovu *Zimbabwe*	34
Riyad Mahrez *Algeria*	27
Stephane Sessegnon *Benin*	25
Lomana LuaLua *DR Congo*	24
Tony Yeboah *Ghana*	24
Mido *Egypt*	22
Joseph-Desire Job *Cameroon*	16
Hassan Kachloul *Morocco*	16
Chris Samba *Congo*	16
Titi Camara *Guinea*	9
Radhi Jaidi *Tunisia*	8
Victor Wanyama *Kenya*	8

Yorke won the 1998-99
Prem Golden Boot award

Kun has got one of the
best goals-to-minute
ratios in Prem history

'S TOP SCORERS
BY COUNTRY!

EUROPE

Player/Country	Goals
Alan Shearer *England*	260
Thierry Henry *France*	175
Robin van Persie *Holland*	144
Robbie Keane *Rep. Of Ireland*	126
Ryan Giggs *Wales*	109
Dimitar Berbatov *Bulgaria*	94
Ole Gunnar Solskjaer *Norway*	91
Romelu Lukaku *Belgium*	85
Fernando Torres *Spain*	85
Cristiano Ronaldo *Portugal*	84
Duncan Ferguson *Scotland*	68
Paolo Di Canio *Italy*	66
Eidur Gudjohnsen *Iceland*	55
Edin Dzeko *Bosnia & Herzegovina*	50
Freddie Ljungberg *Sweden*	48
Andrei Kanchelskis *Russia*	42

Newcastle legend Shearer is the Prem's greatest ever goalscorer

ASIA/OCEANIA

Player/Country	Goals
Mark Viduka *Australia*	92
Ji-Sung Park *South Korea*	19
Ryan Nelsen *New Zealand*	9
Shinji Okazaki *Japan*	8
Ashkan Dejagah *Iran*	5

Player/Country	Goals
Marian Pahars *Latvia*	42
Patrik Berger *Czech Republic*	38
Mikael Forssell *Finland*	34
Muzzy Izzet *Turkey*	34
Iain Dowie *Northern Ireland*	33
Nicklas Bendtner *Denmark*	32
Yossi Benayoun *Israel*	31
Nikica Jelavic *Croatia*	29
Jurgen Klinsmann *Germany*	29
Savo Milosevic *Serbia*	29
Szilard Nemeth *Slovakia*	23
Dan Petrescu *Romania*	23
Marko Arnautovic *Austria*	22
Stelios Giannakopoulos *Greece*	20
Zoltan Gera *Hungary*	17
Serhiy Rebrov *Ukraine*	10

Drog won the Prem title four times in total

Viduka played for three Prem clubs - Newcastle, Middlesbrough & Leeds

Stats correct up to the start of the 2017-18 season.

BEST YouTube CLIPS OF 2017!

MATCH REVEALS THE COOLEST AND FUNNIEST FOOTY VIDEOS WE'VE SEEN THIS YEAR! CHECK THEM OUT...

QR CODE EXPLAINED

This is a QR code – just scan it with your phone or tablet to watch each video clip on YouTube. Here's how to do it:

 Download and install a free QR Code reader from the app or android store.

 Hold your phone or tablet over the QR code and you'll be sent to the clip. Easy!

LOL FIFA GLITCHES... PART TWO

F2Freestylers

At the end of 2016, our mates The F2 recreated a compilation of FIFA glitches in real life. Well, they did it again in 2017 and we couldn't stop laughing! The LOL outtakes at the end are proper side-splitting!

▶ ALEXIS EMBARRASSED

Sportdude

Alexis Sanchez is normally the one busting out cool tricks, but in this clip he gets owned by Gabriel, who nutmegs him with an ace no-look pass! When Sanchez realises it's all caught on camera, he loses it!

▶ CHAMPO LEAGUE LEGO RE-CAP

My Funny Games Builder

Seeing Real Madrid beat Juventus to win their 12th Champo League crown was great to watch in real life, and the showdown re-created in LEGO is nearly as good! Cristiano Ronaldo totally rocks in brick form!

▶ ROOFTOP TEKKERS

Jimmy Kimmel Live

Neymar is no stranger to wondergoals, but you won't have seen him score many like this! He hits a sweet strike from one roof into a net on another roof across the street. Wow!

▶ RONALDINHO SKILL-SHOCKED

PSG

Freestyler Lisa Zimouche hid a camera, then wowed Ronaldinho with her jaw-dropping tricks at PSG's Parc des Princes! Ron was so impressed, he had to join in and bust out some of his own tekkers!

▶ CHELSEA'S FIFA CHALLENGE

EA SPORTS FIFA

Chelsea's Belgium stars Hazard, Batshuayi and Courtois teamed up against a Rest Of The World trio including Chalobah, Zouma and Kante to see who could bag more points in a real-life FIFA bucket challenge!

▶ BARÇA'S EMOJI FUNNIES

FC Barcelona

Before he left for PSG, Barcelona asked Neymar and his Samba mate Rafinha to sum up the Barça players using just Emojis! The Brazilian duo couldn't stop laughing - especially when picking for each other!

▶ DAB BEEN DITCHED?

Timi dapsin

Man. United megastars Paul Pogba and Jesse Lingard showed off their new celebration with dance moves to WizKid's 'Hush Up The Silence' in this clip! The moves are slick, fellas - but we still prefer The Dab!

HE SAID WHAT?

Get a load of some of our fave football quotes from 2017!

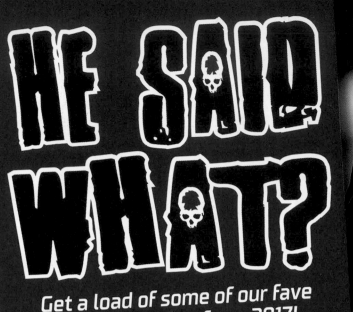

"I'VE KEPT IT QUIET FOR THE LAST 13 YEARS, BUT I'VE ACTUALLY BEEN WEARING EVERTON PYJAMAS AT HOME WITH MY KIDS!"

After returning to his childhood club, Wayne Rooney reveals Everton were always the team for him!

"THE BEST SONG? DON'T LAUGH, BUT I LIKE WHITNEY HOUSTON!"

Celtic defender *Kolo Toure* gets a bit mixed up when asked for his favourite song he's heard from fans during his career!

"I'VE WATCHED ALL THE CHAMPIONS LEAGUE AND EURO 2016 MATCHES AGAIN, BUT I STOPPED AT THE SEMI-FINALS!"

Atletico Madrid and France forward *Antoine Griezmann* still isn't over his two final defeats in the summer of 2016!

"THAT'S NEVER HAPPENED TO ME – A GUY SLEEPING IN THE PRESS CONFERENCE! I MUST HAVE BEEN BORING! GOOD MORNING, EH!"

Ex-Barça gaffer *Luis Enrique* sees the funny side of a reporter falling asleep during one of his press conferences!

"IF BEATING THEM WAS LIKE GETTING TO THE MOON, DOING SO AFTER GOING BEHIND WOULD BE LIKE GETTING TO PLUTO!"

Lincoln City manager *Danny Cowley* is on another planet after The Imps come from behind to beat Brighton 3-1 in the FA Cup fourth round!

"ON SUNDAYS, I LIKE TO TRY SUNDAY ROAST AND I REALLY LIKE BEEF PIE. THE ONE THING I DIDN'T LIKE WAS FISH AND CHIPS – IT'S VERY FAMOUS, BUT IT'S A BIT OILY!"

Man. United midfielder *Juan Mata* isn't a fan of a Friday night chippy!

MATCH!
WEBSITE

Our awesome footy site features all this mind-blowing stuff...

WORLD STARS
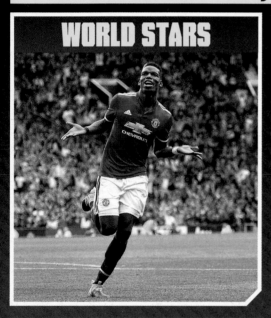

FIFA TIPS

EPIC VIDEOS

COOL QUIZZES
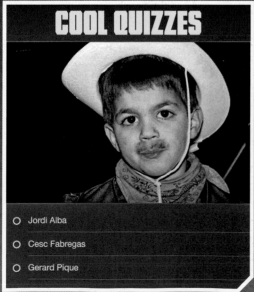

○ Jordi Alba
○ Cesc Fabregas
○ Gerard Pique

SKILLS ADVICE
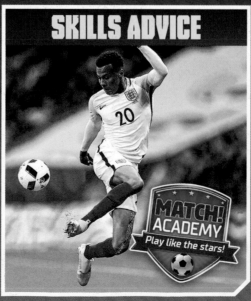

& LOADS MORE!

GO TO WWW.MATCHFOOTBALL.CO.UK

2018'S A BIG YEAR FOR...
LACAZETTE

Can the goal king fire The Gunners to the title?

THE STORY SO FAR...

The ice-cool finisher joined his hometown club Lyon when he was just 12 years old! His goals for the youth team, as well as the reserve side, made him a well-known talent before he made his full debut for the club as an 18-year-old in May 2010!

For his first few years, Lacazette was played out wide, but in 2013-14 he was shifted up front and found his goalscoring boots! The following year his form took off, and he ended the season as Ligue 1's top scorer and Player Of The Season!

After he hit 100 Ligue 1 goals in his final game for Lyon, Arsenal finally made their move for Laca – years after first scouting him! The Gunners spent £46.5 million to make him their most expensive player ever – will he live up to his price tag in 2018?

CL CHASE

This season is the first time Arsenal haven't been in the CL since gaffer Arsene Wenger arrived at the club, and Lacazette has been signed to get the Prem giants straight back into the big-time! Whether it's through a top-four finish or victory in the Europa League, the hitman needs to fire The Gunners back into Europe's elite competition!

TROPHY TIME

The France goal machine's trophy cabinet has only got a couple of domestic cups in it from his time at Lyon, so he says he's moved to North London to win major titles! The lightning-fast striker needs to score goals to make sure The Gunners are challenging for the top honours - can he deliver more silverware to The Emirates?

FRENCH FLAIR

Arsenal have a massive tradition when it comes to French forwards, and the new No.9 will be under big pressure to follow in their footsteps! In their first seasons at the club, Sylvain Wiltord ripped net 15 times in all comps, Olivier Giroud got 17, and Thierry Henry hit 26! Where will Lacazette rank after his first season in English football?

LES BLEUS BATTLE

France's strength in depth is ridiculous, and Lacazette has a serious battle on his hands to make it into their World Cup squad! He's been kept out of the side by Olivier Giroud and Antoine Griezmann recently, and with Kylian Mbappe, Ousmane Dembele and Anthony Martial to compete with too, he'll need to be on top form!

2018 IN NUMBERS...

4
Lacazette is chasing a fourth consecutive season of scoring over 20 league goals!

9
If he does, he'll be the first Arsenal No.9 to get 20 goals in a Prem season!

1
Russia 2018 will be his first-ever senior international tournament – if he gets picked!

150
The world-class finisher could bag his 150th career goal in 2018!

BIG MATCH! QUIZ

EFL SPECIAL

YouTube STAR!

Which Championship new boy has taken the place of Billy from The F2?

MATCH MATHS!

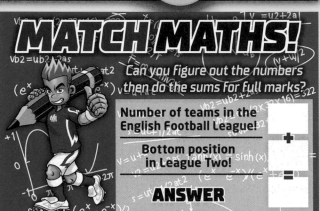

Can you figure out the numbers then do the sums for full marks?

Number of teams in the English Football League!	
+	
Bottom position in League Two!	
=	
ANSWER	

THE NICKNAME GAME!

MATCH these class League One clubs with their crazy nicknames!

Southend	Blackpool	Bristol Rovers	Scunthorpe
1	2	3	4
A	B	C	D
The Pirates	The Shrimpers	The Iron	The Seasiders

FREAKY FACES!

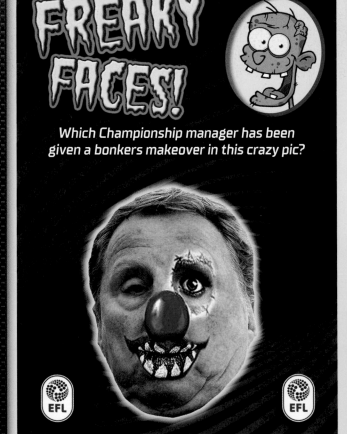

Which Championship manager has been given a bonkers makeover in this crazy pic?

GROUNDED!

Which League Two team play their home games at Meadow Lane?

FOOTY MIS-MATCH

Spot the ten differences between these play-off pics!

1	6
2	7
3	8
4	9
5	10

ANSWERS ON PAGE 94

EFL BRAIN-BUSTER!

How much do you know about the EFL? Find out...

1. Chelsea striker Tammy Abraham is on loan at Swansea this season, but which EFL club did he play for in 2016-17?

2. Which of these teams didn't win promotion in the 2016-17 season – Preston, Plymouth or Portsmouth?

3. Two ex-Premier League champions hold the record for winning England's second tier the most times – name them!

4. Which League One club plays their home games at Valley Parade?

Pos.		P	W	D	L	GD	Pts
1	Newcastle United	46	29	7	10	45	94
2	Brighton and Hove Albion	46	28	9	9	25	93
3	Reading	46	26	7	13	4	85
4	Sheffield Wednesday	46	24	9	13	15	81
5	Huddersfield Town	46	25	6	15	-2	81
6	Fulham	46	22	14	10	29	80
7	Leeds United	46	22	9	15	14	75
8	Norwich City	46	20	10	16	10	70
9	Derby County	46	18	13	15	4	67
10	Brentford	46	18	10	18	10	64
11	Preston North End	46	16	14	16	1	62

5. Which team finished second in the Championship in the 2016-17 season?

6. Dele Alli joined Tottenham from which League One club in 2015?

7. Which team has the biggest stadium in the Championship?

8. Billy Sharp was the top scorer in the Football League last season, but which club did he score his 30 goals for?

9. Which League Two club is playing in the English Football League for the very first time this season?

10. How many teams take part in the EFL play-offs at the end of every season – four, six or 12?

1 ....
2 ....
3 ....
4 ....
5 ....
6 ....
7 ....
8 ....
9 ....
10 ....

ANSWERS ON PAGE 94

Standard Chartered

L.F.C.
125 YEARS
1892 2017

FIRMINO

FAB FACT
During his youth career in Brazil, the Liverpool hitman played as a defensive midfielder. Mad!

BOOTS
adidas Nemeziz 17+

STAT ATTACK
The Samba star bagged over 20 goals and assists combined in all comps last season for The Reds!

TRANSFER VALUE

£55 MILLION

ULTIMATE TEAM LEGENDS EXPLAINED!

With the release of brand-new FUT Icons on FIFA 18, MATCH takes a closer look at what made some past Legends on FIFA's Ultimate Team so legendary!

SCHOLES
CM ★ OVR 89

Paul Scholes dominated tons of games for Man. United from his debut in 1994 until he retired in 2013! The midfield maestro originally quit the game in 2011, but returned a year later! With the epic playmaker back in the team, The Red Devils bossed the 2012-13 season as he lifted his 11th Prem title!

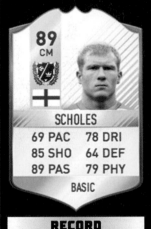

89 CM
SCHOLES
69 PAC	78 DRI
85 SHO	64 DEF
89 PAS	79 PHY

BASIC

RECORD	
International Games	66
International Goals	14
League Games	499
League Goals	107
Major Trophies	25

BEST
RW ★ OVR 90

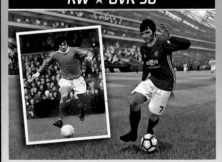

The history of United's legendary No.7 shirt all started with George Best! The Northern Irishman wowed Old Trafford with his silky dribbling skills, and his partnership with United heroes Bobby Charlton and Denis Law helped them become the first English side to win the CL, with Best scoring in the final!

90 RW
BEST
90 PAC	94 DRI
89 SHO	59 DEF
81 PAS	68 PHY

BASIC

RECORD	
International Games	37
International Goals	9
League Games	604
League Goals	239
Major Trophies	5

NESTA
CB ★ OVR 90

Italy have produced some of the world's best ever CBs, and Alessandro Nesta is definitely one of them! The ex-Serie A superstar had the power and timing in his tackles to win the ball back, and the technical ability to play quality passes. At AC Milan, he won two league titles and two Champions Leagues. Hero!

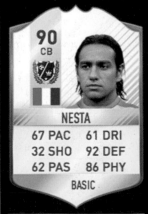

90 CB
NESTA
67 PAC	61 DRI
32 SHO	92 DEF
62 PAS	86 PHY

BASIC

RECORD	
International Games	78
International Goals	0
League Games	451
League Goals	8
Major Trophies	18

CANNAVARO
CB ★ OVR 89

Fabio Cannavaro made his name at Parma, Juventus and Real Madrid, but his greatest moment came in an Italy shirt. After being made The Azzurri captain, he inspired his team to 2006 World Cup glory! His displays helped him bag the Ballon d'Or – and he's still the last defender to win the award!

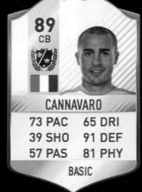

89
CB
CANNAVARO

73 PAC	65 DRI
39 SHO	91 DEF
57 PAS	81 PHY

BASIC

RECORD

International Games	136
International Goals	2
League Games	531
League Goals	16
Major Trophies	8

CRESPO
ST ★ OVR 87

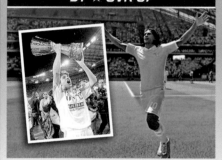

87
ST
CRESPO

87 PAC	80 DRI
86 SHO	25 DEF
69 PAS	69 PHY

BASIC

Hernan Crespo's technical ability and lethal finishing made him a world-class striker, and convinced Lazio to splash £35 million on him – a world record in 2000! More big moves to Chelsea and Inter made him the first player to rack up over £100 million in combined fees, and he won both the Prem and Serie A!

RECORD

International Games	64
International Goals	35
League Games	453
League Goals	198
Major Trophies	15

FIGO
RW ★ OVR 90

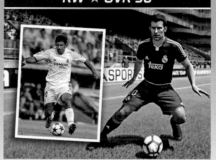

90
RW
FIGO

83 PAC	90 DRI
81 SHO	38 DEF
86 PAS	75 PHY

BASIC

Luis Figo is often remembered for his controversial transfer from Barça to Real Madrid, but he was one of the best wingers European footy's ever seen! Only Lionel Messi has more La Liga assists than the top dribbler, who tied defenders in knots with his stepovers and turn of pace. He was top class!

RECORD

International Games	127
International Goals	32
League Games	577
League Goals	93
Major Trophies	22

LINEKER
ST ★ OVR 89

Before he became a top presenter, Gary Lineker was a goal machine! He banged loads in for Leicester and Everton, before bagging the Golden Boot at the 1986 World Cup! He's the last Englishman to play for Barcelona, and only two players have scored more goals for The Three Lions!

89
ST
LINEKER

86 PAC	80 DRI
87 SHO	28 DEF
69 PAS	75 PHY

BASIC

RECORD

International Games	80
International Goals	48
League Games	460
League Goals	238
Major Trophies	4

NEDVED
LM ★ OVR 89

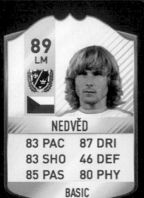

89
LM

NEDVĚD

83 PAC	87 DRI
83 SHO	46 DEF
85 PAS	80 PHY

BASIC

Pavel Nedved burst onto the world stage as a star of the Czech Republic team that reached the final of Euro '96. Totally two-footed, his lethal long shots and excellent passing range made him a threat across the pitch! In 2003, he beat Thierry Henry and Paolo Maldini to the Ballon d'Or. What a player!

RECORD

International Games	91
International Goals	18
League Games	501
League Goals	110
Major Trophies	15

OWEN
ST ★ OVR 88

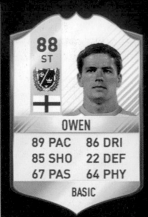

88
ST

OWEN

89 PAC	86 DRI
85 SHO	22 DEF
67 PAS	64 PHY

BASIC

Michael Owen was a natural-born scorer with electric pace and lethal finishing! After exploding into Liverpool's first team as a teenager, he went on to play for huge clubs Real Madrid, Newcastle and Man. United! MATCH reckons he'd be England's record goalscorer if he hadn't picked up so many injuries!

RECORD

International Games	89
International Goals	40
League Games	362
League Goals	163
Major Trophies	9

SEAMAN
GK ★ OVR 88

88
GK

SEAMAN

78 DIV	85 REF
90 HAN	50 SPE
93 KIC	88 POS

BASIC

13 years and 564 appearances for Arsenal mean GK David Seaman is a proper Gunners legend! After moving to Highbury in 1990, he was one of the best goalkeepers in the Prem for over a decade! You have to YouTube his wondersave against Sheffield United in the 2003 FA Cup – it's sensational!

RECORD

International Games	75
International Goals	0
League Games	731
League Goals	0
Major Trophies	12

SHEARER
ST ★ OVR 89

89
ST

SHEARER

78 PAC	76 DRI
90 SHO	50 DEF
77 PAS	84 PHY

BASIC

With monster power and a rocket right foot, Alan Shearer was unstoppable! Throughout his legendary career, he scored long-range thunderbolts, bullet headers and goal poacher's tap-ins! Not only has the Magpies man scored more Premier League goals than anyone else, he's got more hat-tricks too!

RECORD

International Games	63
International Goals	30
League Games	559
League Goals	283
Major Trophies	1

VAN NISTELROOY
ST ★ OVR 90

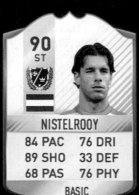

90
ST

NISTELROOY

84 PAC	76 DRI
89 SHO	33 DEF
68 PAS	76 PHY

BASIC

Ruud van Nistelrooy was a proper predator who just loved scoring goals! After joining Man. United from PSV in 2001, he ripped 95 Prem nets for The Red Devils, but hardly ever from outside the penalty area! His lethal finishing helped him bag five league titles in England, Spain and Holland!

RECORD

International Games	70
International Goals	35
League Games	449
League Goals	249
Major Trophies	10

GIGGS
LM ★ OVR 89

Ryan Giggs terrorised right-backs for years with his lightning-fast dribbling and lethal left foot! As he got older and slowed down, the Welsh wizard was shifted into central midfield, but remained a key man as United won four Prem titles from 2008 to 2013 to add to the nine already in his cabinet!

89 LM
GIGGS

90 PAC	88 DRI
78 SHO	41 DEF
87 PAS	67 PHY

BASIC

RECORD

International Games	64
International Goals	12
League Games	672
League Goals	114
Major Trophies	34

DEL PIERO
CF ★ OVR 90

90 CF
DEL PIERO

85 PAC	92 DRI
89 SHO	42 DEF
85 PAS	69 PHY

BASIC

Italian football fans describe creative No.10s as 'Trequartistas', and not many players have fitted that description better than Alessandro Del Piero! The Juve legend was a joy to watch, with epic close control, bags of skill and the potential to score spectacular goals! He's one of Italy's all-time top scorers!

RECORD

International Games	91
International Goals	27
League Games	585
League Goals	234
Major Trophies	16

SHEVCHENKO
ST ★ OVR 88

88 ST
SHEVCHENKO

84 PAC	84 DRI
87 SHO	33 DEF
71 PAS	73 PHY

BASIC

Prem fans might remember Andriy Shevchenko as a £30 million flop, but he was the best striker in the world before joining Chelsea! He was a goal machine at AC Milan, finishing top of the Serie A scoring charts twice, and scored their winning penalty in the 2003 Champions League Final!

RECORD

International Games	111
International Goals	48
League Games	446
League Goals	219
Major Trophies	18

LARSSON
ST ★ OVR 87

Celtic got one of the best deals ever when they signed Henrik Larsson for £650,000! From tap-ins to long-range screamers, the Sweden star was lethal - despite injuries threatening his career! After firing The Hoops to a Europa League final, he joined Barça and won the CL with two assists in the final!

87 ST
LARSSON

84 PAC	84 DRI
85 SHO	44 DEF
73 PAS	67 PHY

BASIC

RECORD

International Games	106
International Goals	37
League Games	576
League Goals	325
Major Trophies	16

RU 2 BROTHERS?

Were these footy superstars separated from these celebrities at birth?

MANNY
YOUTUBE VLOGGER

MY VIDEOS ARE WAY BETTER!

OUSMANE DEMBELE
BARCELONA SPEEDSTER

LIAM PAYNE
MUSIC MEGASTAR

AARON RAMSEY
ARSENAL MIDFIELD MASTER

FANCY FEATURING ON MY NEXT TRACK?

NICK JONAS
AMERICAN SINGER

LIAM HEMSWORTH
AUSTRALIAN ACTOR

GERARD PIQUE
BARCELONA ROCK

BOGUS BEARD ALERT!

IT'S A MIRROR IMAGE!

EDEN HAZARD
CHELSEA WING WIZARD

ARE WE LONG LOST TWINS?

RYAN GOSLING
CANADIAN ACTOR

HARRY KANE
TOTTENHAM GOAL KING

CAN I REPLACE VIN DIESEL, MATE?

82 MATCH!

MATCH!
THE BEST FOOTBALL MAGAZINE!

HAZARD

YOKOHAMA TYRES

FAB FACT
The wicked winger has won Chelsea's Goal Of The Season award for the last two Premier League campaigns. Baller!

BOOTS
Nike Mercurial

STAT ATTACK
Hazard was one of only two players to be fouled more than 100 times in the Premier League last season!

TRANSFER VALUE
£90 MILLION

SNAPPED!
BEST OF 2017!

Super Auba!

Trust us, that's Aubameyang under that superhero mask!

Land of the Giants!

Talk about a mis-match!

Cheeky Costa!

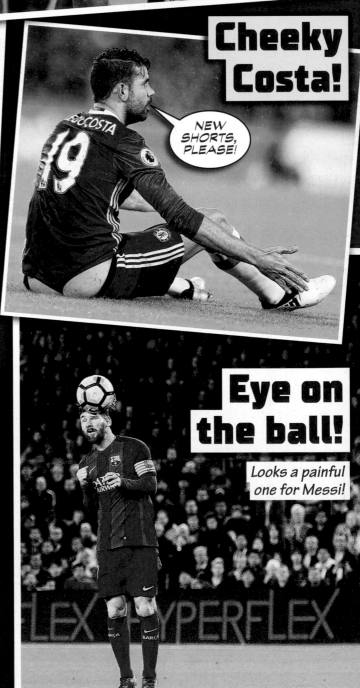

Eye on the ball!

Looks a painful one for Messi!

Guff alert!

> PARDON ME!

Pickford just can't hold it in!

Crowd surfer!

JT thinks he's at a music gig!

> LET'S SWAP SHIRTS!

> OI, GET OFF ME!

You're going nowhere!

Herrera takes man-marking well seriously!

Double trouble!

Quick, get the physios on!

> AM I GETTING DOUBLE VISION?

> STRETCHER, PLEASE!

> I'M GOING FIRST!

> NO CHANCE, MATE!

> CABBA WINS EASY!

Slaphead showdown!

Caballero and Pep argue whose hairstyle's better!

Gurn copycat!

Kane does his best Jones gurn impression!

TOP 10 FOOTBALL UNDERDOGS!

Check out MATCH's fave David versus Goliath footy moments!

10
BANTAMS BEAT BLUES!
Chelsea 2-4 Bradford
FA Cup, January 2015

Nobody gave League One Bradford a chance against top-of-the-table Chelsea before this fourth round tie, let alone when they went 2-0 down! The Bantams never quit though, and four epic goals later they'd pulled off one of the greatest ever FA Cup upsets!

9
WC HOLDERS STUNNED!
Argentina 0-1 Cameroon
World Cup 1990

In this underdog tale, reigning champs Argentina, led by footy legend Diego Maradona, were stunned by unfancied Cameroon in the opening game of the 1990 World Cup! It was a result not only celebrated by Cameroon fans, but the whole of Africa!

7
SUNDERLAND IN DREAM LAND!
Sunderland 1-0 Leeds
1973 FA Cup Final

FA Cup holders Leeds against second division Sunderland - only one winner right? Wrong! The Black Cats stunned the then English giants with a heroic Wembley display. Gaffer Bob Stokoe's famous run onto the pitch at full-time has even been turned into a statue outside the Stadium Of Light!

8
SAINTS SLAY RED DEVILS!
Man. United 0-1 Southampton
1976 FA Cup Final

This was another case of a plucky lower league side beating a top-flight team! The Red Devils had finished third in 1976 while in the division below, The Saints ended the season in sixth. The south-coast side shocked United in front of nearly 100,000 fans to bag their first ever major trophy!

6
NON-LEAGUE LEGENDS!
Hereford 2-1 Newcastle
FA Cup, February 1972

If 'FA Cup Giantkilling' was in the dictionary, this game would be staring right back at you! A non-league side beating a top-flight team in a third-round replay, and doing so with one of the competition's greatest ever goals - it's the stuff dreams are made of!

5 THREE LIONS FROZEN OUT!
England 1-2 Iceland Euro 2016

Coached by a dentist and with a film director in goal, Iceland handed The Three Lions their worst ever defeat in Nice! England led early on, but by the 18th minute were 2-1 down. They couldn't find an equaliser, and the Icelandic thunder-clappers went through to the quarter-finals. Ouch!

4

GREEK GODS!
Portugal 0-1 Greece Euro 2004 Final

Greece stunned the footy world when they became Euro champs in only their third major tournament! They got out of a tough group which included Spain and Portugal, beat reigning champions France, and then stunned Cristiano Ronaldo and co. again in the final!

3

DEADLY DANES!
Denmark 2-0 Germany Euro 1992 Final

How does a country who didn't even qualify for the tournament end up bagging the trophy? Well… after one team got banned, Denmark were called in to make up the numbers. The Danes did more than that though, and became champions of Europe for the first time!

2

FANTASTIC FOXES!
Leicester win the title 2015-16 Premier League

In a league dominated by the big-spending clubs, and with a boss who'd never won a top-flight title in his career, Leicester somehow won the Prem - despite nearly getting relegated the year before! It's the biggest shock in the Premier League era!

1

FOREST THE KINGS OF EUROPE!
Nottingham Forest win the title then European Cup twice 1978-80

Imagine an underdog surprising everyone like Leicester did, then going on to win the Champo League two seasons in a row! Well, that's exactly what Nottingham Forest did! In 1977 they got promoted to the top flight, but by 1980 they'd won a league title and added two CLs to their trophy cabinet!

2018'S A BIG YEAR FOR...

LUKAKU

Can Rom become The Red Devils' main man in 2018?

THE STORY SO FAR...

Lukaku exploded onto the scene while in Anderlecht's academy as a teenager, making a name for himself before he'd even played a first-team game! His record of 131 goals in 93 academy games convinced the club to give him his debut aged just 16!

After 33 goals in 73 league games, Chelsea paid £18 million for Romelu in 2011, hoping he'd become their new Didier Drogba. It was on loan at West Brom and Everton where he proved himself as a star though, with The Toffees paying £28 million for Rom in 2014!

53 Prem goals later, Lukaku was once again in demand in the summer of 2017. After a battle between his old club Chelsea and Man. United, The Red Devils finally won the race for his signature, and paid £75 million to sign him! Will he be worth the money?

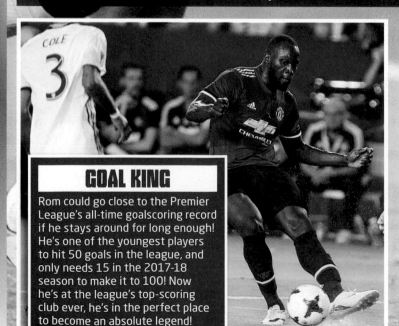

GOAL KING

Rom could go close to the Premier League's all-time goalscoring record if he stays around for long enough! He's one of the youngest players to hit 50 goals in the league, and only needs 15 in the 2017-18 season to make it to 100! Now he's at the league's top-scoring club ever, he's in the perfect place to become an absolute legend!

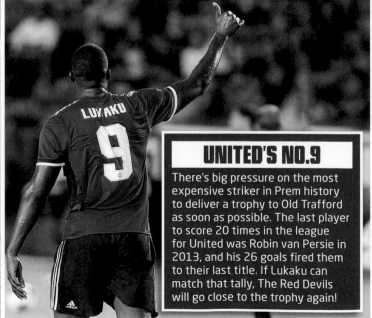

UNITED'S NO.9

There's big pressure on the most expensive striker in Prem history to deliver a trophy to Old Trafford as soon as possible. The last player to score 20 times in the league for United was Robin van Persie in 2013, and his 26 goals fired them to their last title. If Lukaku can match that tally, The Red Devils will go close to the trophy again!

CL CHALLENGE

Luk's been talking about playing in the Champions League for ages, but this is his first season taking on Europe's top clubs since he featured in the qualifying rounds for Anderlecht way back in 2010. The Belgium beast needs to prove himself in the latter stages of the competition to prove that he's worth his massive price tag!

BELGIUM BID

Russia 2018 will be Lukaku's third major tournament, but neither he nor his team-mates have ever really fulfilled their huge potential on the international stage. With stars like Eden Hazard, Kevin De Bruyne and Mousa Dembele supporting the big man up front, surely this will be the tournament where Belgium and Lukaku make their mark?

2018 IN NUMBERS...

30
Lukaku will be aiming to end his debut season with a personal best of 30 goals in all comps!

4
If he reaches 100 Prem goals, he'll be the fourth youngest player to bag a century!

1
His only trophy in England is Chelsea's 2012 FA Cup win – he needs to add more!

30
The lethal finisher isn't far off Belgium's all-time goalscoring record of 30!

WIN! ACE FOOTY BUNDLE!

Thanks to our top mates at Sports Direct, we've got a wicked collection of football gear up for grabs! One MATCH Annual 2018 reader will win all this...

★ England Home Shirt
★ Nike Pitch Football
★ Sondico Neosa Goalkeeper Gloves
★ Puma Spirit Ankle Shin Guards

CLOSING DATE: JAN. 31 2018

Head to SportsDirect.com for tons more quality footy gear!

SPORTS DIRECT.com

EPIC STEALTH 700 GAMING HEADSETS!

Turtle Beach are giving away these cool Stealth 700 gaming headsets - one for Xbox One and one for PlayStation4!

The Stealth 700 gaming headset features an all-new modern style and delivers immersive surround sound and chat audio through powerful 50mm over-ear speakers! For loads more info, check out www.turtlebeach.com

2 PRIZES!

TURTLE BEACH®

CLOSING DATE: JAN. 31 2018

HOW TO ENTER!  **WWW.MATCHFOOTBALL.CO.UK**

Then click 'Win' in the navigation bar on the MATCH website. Full T&Cs are available online.

KANE

NIKE AEROSWIFT

FAB FACT

The England striker hit 36% of the hat-tricks scored in the 2016-17 Premier League season!

BOOTS

Nike Hypervenom

STAT ATTACK

No player has bagged more Prem goals in the last three seasons than Tottenham's lethal finisher. Ledge!

TRANSFER VALUE

£90 MILLION

FREE ISSUE OF MATCH! FOR EVERY READER!

5 FREE POSTERS!

GET THEM EVERY WEEK!

MAHREZ

COUTINHO

DI MARIA

NEYMAR

MATCH

GIANT POSTER

NEYMAR

FAB FACT!

MATCH SKILL KINGS

4 SKILL KINGS MEGA POSTERS

MAHREZ

COUTINHO

LANNIN

DI MARIA

BAL

MASSIVE INT THE REAL

PLUS... CHAMPIONS LEAGUE SEMI-FINAL PREVIEWS!

FREE MAG WORTH £2.25!

AW NE

8 EPIC GIFTS

ROAD TO 2018 FIFA WORLD CUP™ GIFTS

ROAD TO 2018 FIFA WORLD CUP RUSSIA

OFFICIAL LICENSED

STICKER ALBUM

STICKER ALBUM

2 PACKS OF STICKERS

PANINI

MATCH!

JUNE 6-12 2017 ISSUE NO: 1927

£2.99

9 770955 494988

23

GIANT POSTER

GRIEZMANN

4 CRAZY MEGA POSTERS

AUBAMEYANG

WORLD CUP SPECIAL! Scotland v England, Rashford interview, 2018 qualifiers & more!

PLAY LIKE...

DELE ALLI

PLUS INSIDE!

★ FIFA 18 wish list
★ Hot transfer gossip
★ City new boy Bernardo

NEW GEAR!
★ Messi's kicks
★ Adidas boots
★ 6 new kits & more!

GUESS WHO INSTAGRAM GONE MAD!

YOU'RE 'GUNNER' FIND OUT INSIDE!

WIN! ▶ MAN. CITY SHIRT ▶ 2017-18 EFL BALL ▶ TRAIN WITH A TOP PREM CLUB

*Album not available to subscribers. †Album and stickers not available overseas. Stickers may differ from those shown.

92 MATCH!

PACKED EVERY WEEK WITH...

MASSIVE STARS

RED-HOT GEAR

STATS & FACTS

FIFA 18 TIPS

EPIC QUIZZES

LOL PICS & LOADS MORE!

TO CLAIM YOUR FREE COPY OF MATCH...
CALL 0800 923 3006 QUOTE: MATT103

QUIZ ANSWERS!

Prem Quiz   Pages 18-20

Sport Switch: Harry Kane.

Arsenal Quiz: 1. The Gunners; 2. 13;
3. Tottenham; 4. Over 60,000; 5. No.14.

Close-Up:
1. Gabriel Jesus; 2. Chris Brunt;
3. Seamus Coleman; 4. Charlie Austin.

Soccer Scrabble: Bernardo Silva.

Name The Team: 1. Eden Hazard;
2. David Luiz; 3. John Terry; 4. Thibaut
Courtois; 5. Diego Costa; 6. N'Golo Kante;
7. Victor Moses; 8. Cesc Fabregas;
9. Cesar Azpilicueta; 10. Willian.

Super Skippers:
Man. City - Vincent Kompany; Liverpool
- Jordan Henderson; Tottenham - Hugo
Lloris; West Ham - Mark Noble.

Goal Machines: 1. Bournemouth;
2. Crystal Palace; 3. Arsenal; 4. Stoke;
5. Newcastle; 6. Huddersfield.

MATCH Winner: Fernando Llorente

Wicked Wordfit: See below.

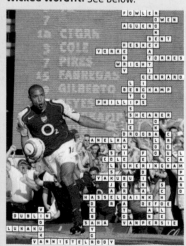

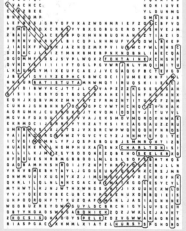

WC Quiz   Pages 34-36

Odd One Out: Holland.

Flipped: Pepe.

Crazy Kit: Australia.

Mega Mash-Up: Hector Bellerin.

Stadium Game: 1-C; 2-B; 3-D; 4-A.

Spot The Ball: C8.

Guess The Winners:
2010 - Spain; 2006 - Italy;
2002 - Brazil; 1998 - France.

World Cup Stoppers: 1. Germany;
2. England; 3. Sweden; 4. Trinidad
& Tobago; 5. Holland; 6. Portugal.

MATCH Winner: Mario Gotze.

Mega Wordsearch: See below.

CL Quiz   Pages 58-60

Footy At The Films: Luis Suarez.

Back To The Future: Gareth Bale.

Spot The Sponsor:
1. Monaco; 2. Dortmund; 3. Barcelona;
4. Juventus; 5. Chelsea; 6. PSG.

Beardy Weirdy: 1. Isco; 2. Juan
Mata; 3. Daniele De Rossi; 4. Gabi.

Camera Shy: Pierre-E. Aubameyang,
Christian Eriksen & Miralem Pjanic.

Action Replay: 1. 4-1; 2. Khedira;
3. Ronaldo; 4. Under five; 5. Benzema;
6. 27; 7. Real Madrid; 8. Cuadrado.

Spot The Stars: See above.

EFL Quiz   Pages 74-76

YouTube Star: George Boyd.

MATCH Maths: 72 + 24 = 96.

Nickname Game: 1-B; 2-D; 3-A; 4-C.

Freaky Faces: Harry Redknapp.

Grounded: Notts County.

Footy Mis-Match: See above.

Brain-Buster: 1. Bristol City; 2. Preston;
3. Leicester & Man. City; 4. Bradford;
5. Brighton; 6. MK Dons; 7. Sunderland;
8. Sheff. United; 9. Forest Green; 10. 12.

**Give yourself one point
for each correct answer!**

SCORE   /204